EUROPE

World Continents Series

Written by David McAleese and Irene Evagelelis

GRADES 5 - 8

Reading Levels 3 - 4

Classroom Complete Press
P.O. Box 19729
San Diego, CA 92159
Tel: 1-800-663-3609 | Fax: 1-800-663-3608
Email: service@classroomcompletepress.com

www.classroomcompletepress.com

ISBN-13: 978-1-55319-310-5
ISBN-10: 1-55319-310-4

Critical Thinking Skills

Europe

Level	Skills For Critical Thinking	Reading Comprehension: Location	Place	Human & Environment Interactions	Movement	Regions
LEVEL 1 Knowledge	• Match	✓			✓	✓
	• Show or Label	✓	✓			
	• List Information	✓			✓	
	• Recall Details (5Ws + H)	✓	✓	✓	✓	✓
	• Find Information	✓	✓	✓	✓	
LEVEL 2 Comprehension	• Describe & Compare	✓				
	• Summarize	✓		✓	✓	
	• Explain			✓		
	• Select					✓
LEVEL 3 Application	• Organize Information	✓		✓	✓	✓
	• Interview		✓	✓		
	• Apply	✓		✓	✓	✓
LEVEL 4 Analysis	• Conclude		✓	✓		
	• Analyze			✓		✓
LEVEL 5 Synthesis	• Design				✓	✓
	• Create				✓	✓
LEVEL 6 Evaluation	• Evaluate			✓		✓
	• Compare			✓		✓

Based on Bloom's Taxonomy

Contents

TEACHER GUIDE

- Assessment Rubric 4
- How Is Our Resource Organized? 5
- Bloom's Taxonomy for Reading Comprehension 6
- Vocabulary 6

STUDENT HANDOUTS

- Reading Comprehension – Five Themes of Geography
  - *1. Location* 7
  - *2. Place* 11
  - *3. Human and Environmental Interactions* 16
  - *4. Movement* 20
  - *5. Regions* 24
- Crossword 29
- Word Search 30
- Comprehension Quiz 31

EASY MARKING™ ANSWER KEY 33

STUDENT BLACKLINE MAPS 37

MINI POSTERS 49

Assessment Rubric

Europe

Student's Name: ____________________ Assignment: ____________________ Level: __________

	Level 1	Level 2	Level 3	Level 4
Understanding Concepts	Demonstrates a limited understanding of the concepts. Requires teacher intervention	Demonstrates a basic understanding of the concepts	Demonstrates a good understanding of the concepts	Demonstrates a thorough understanding of the concepts
Response to the Text	Expresses responses to the text with limited effectiveness, inconsistently supported by proof from the text	Expresses responses to the text with some effectiveness, supported by some proof from the text	Expresses responses to the text with appropriate skills, supported with appropriate proof	Expresses thorough and complete responses to the text, supported by concise and effective proof from the text
Application of Own Interests	Interprets and applies various concepts in the text with few, unrelated details and incorrect analysis	Interprets and applies various concepts in the text with some detail, but with some inconsistent analysis	Interprets and applies various concepts in the text with appropriate detail and analysis	Effectively interprets and applies various concepts in the text with consistent, clear and effective detail and analysis

STRENGTHS:

WEAKNESSES:

NEXT STEPS:

Teacher Guide

Our resource has been created for ease of use by both TEACHERS and STUDENTS alike.

Introduction

This resource provides ready-to-use information and activities for remedial students in grades five to eight. Written to grade and using simplified language and vocabulary, geography concepts are presented in a way that makes them more accessible to students and easier to understand. Comprised of reading passages, student activities and mini posters, our resource can be used effectively for whole-class, small group and independent work.

How Is Our Resource Organized?

STUDENT HANDOUTS

Reading passages and **activities** (*in the form of reproducible worksheets*) make up the majority of our resource. The reading passages present important grade-appropriate information and concepts related to the topic. Included in each passage are one or more embedded questions that ensure students are actually reading and understanding the content.

For each reading passage there are **BEFORE YOU READ** activities and **AFTER YOU READ** activities. As with the reading passages, the related activities are written using a remedial level of language.

- The BEFORE YOU READ activities prepare students for reading by setting a purpose for reading. They stimulate background knowledge and experience, and guide students to make connections between what they know and what they will learn. Important concepts and vocabulary from the chapters are also presented.
- The AFTER YOU READ activities check students' comprehension of the concepts presented in the reading passage and extend their learning. Students are asked to give thoughtful consideration of the reading passage through creative and evaluative short-answer questions, research, and extension activities.

Hands-on activities are included to further develop students' thinking skills and understanding of the concepts. The **Assessment Rubric** (*page 4*) is a useful tool for evaluating students' responses to many of the activities in our resource. The **Comprehension Quiz** (*page 31*) can be used for either a follow-up review or assessment at the completion of the unit.

PICTURE CUES

This resource contains three main types of pages, each with a different purpose and use. A **Picture Cue** at the top of each page shows, at a glance, what the page is for.

Teacher Guide
- Information and tools for the teacher

Student Handout
- Reproducible worksheets and activities

Easy Marking™ Answer Key
- Answers for student activities

EASY MARKING™ ANSWER KEY

Marking students' worksheets is fast and easy with this **Answer Key**. Answers are listed in columns – just line up the column with its corresponding worksheet, as shown, and see how every question matches up with its answer!

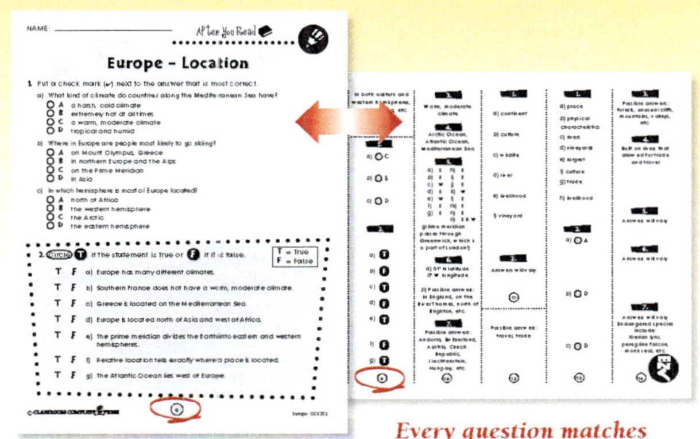

Every question matches up with its answer!

Bloom's Taxonomy

Our resource is an effective tool for any ***GEOGRAPHY PROGRAM.***

Bloom's Taxonomy* for Reading Comprehension

The activities in our resource engage and build the full range of thinking skills that are essential for students' reading comprehension and understanding of important geography concepts. Based on the six levels of thinking in Bloom's Taxonomy, and using language at a remedial level, information and questions are given that challenge students to not only recall what they have read, but move beyond this to understand the text and concepts through higher-order thinking. By using higher-order skills of application, analysis, synthesis and evaluation, students become active readers, drawing more meaning from the text, attaining a greater understanding of concepts, and applying and extending their learning in more sophisticated ways.

Our resource, therefore, is an effective tool for any Geography program. Whether it is used in whole or in part, or adapted to meet individual student needs, our resource provides teachers with essential information and questions to ask, inspiring students' interest, creativity, and promoting meaningful learning.

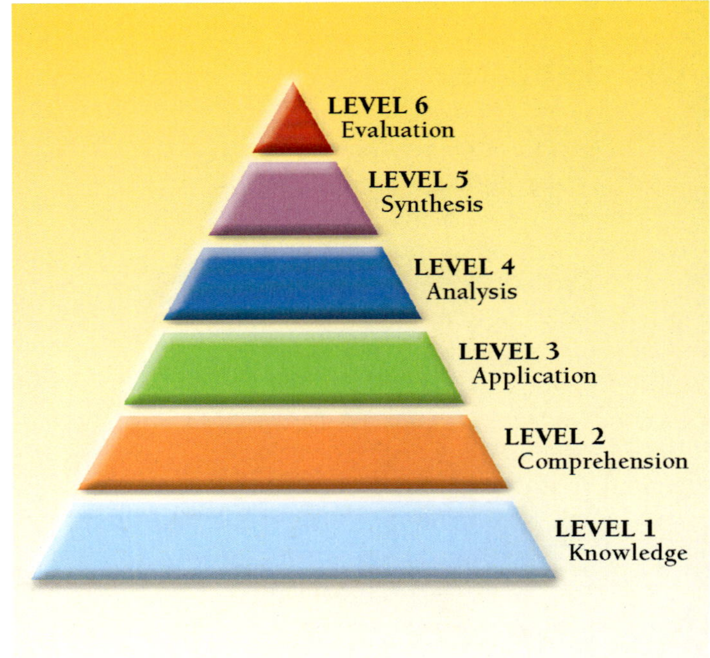

BLOOM'S TAXONOMY: 6 LEVELS OF THINKING

**Bloom's Taxonomy is a widely used tool by educators for classifying learning objectives, and is based on the work of Benjamin Bloom.*

Vocabulary

• hemisphere • prime meridian • latitude • longitude • climate • eastern • western • equator • absolute • exact • relative • location • links • imaginary • continent • boundaries • surround • unique • moderate • extreme • tropical • humid • pleasant • feature • livelihood • vineyard • culture • literature • river • transportation • mountain • coast • interaction • valleys • trade • famous • endangered species • physical • characteristic • wildlife • vegetation • region • fertile • languages • natural resource • population • environment • positive • negative • mineral • preserve • constructive • public • transportation • habitats • pollution • balance • railway • nuclear explosion • radiation • electricity • recycle • communication • geographer • exchanged • vehicles • movement • cruises • automobiles • recreational • electronics • motor • scooters • canal • highway • gondola • mistral winds • lavender • scenery • ancient • peninsula • vacant • orchard • olives • landlocked • conserve

NAME: ______________________________

Europe - Location

1. You be the teacher! Someone has matched the word on the left to the definition on the right. Are they correct? If **yes**, mark it correct with a check mark in the box beside each. If **no**, write an X in the box and correct the work by drawing an arrow to the correct definition. You may use an atlas or a dictionary to help.

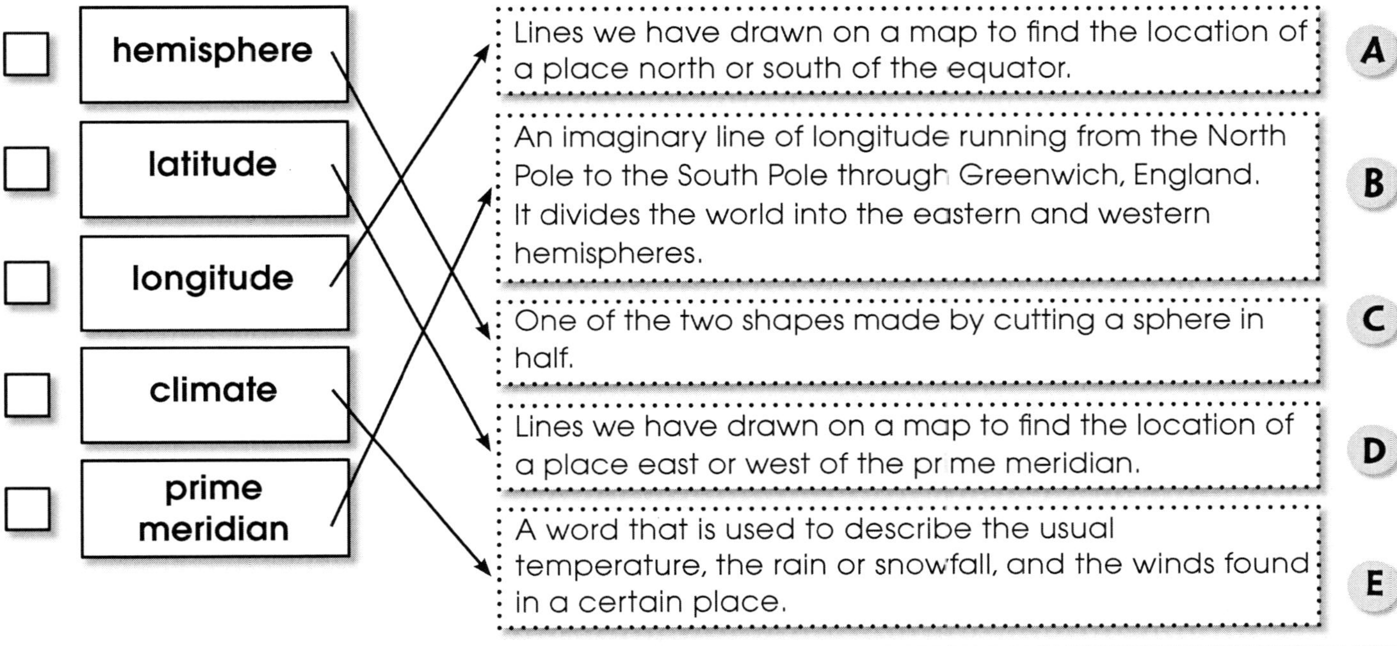

☐ hemisphere

☐ latitude

☐ longitude

☐ climate

☐ prime meridian

A. Lines we have drawn on a map to find the location of a place north or south of the equator.

B. An imaginary line of longitude running from the North Pole to the South Pole through Greenwich, England. It divides the world into the eastern and western hemispheres.

C. One of the two shapes made by cutting a sphere in half.

D. Lines we have drawn on a map to find the location of a place east or west of the prime meridian.

E. A word that is used to describe the usual temperature, the rain or snowfall, and the winds found in a certain place.

2. On the map, show the prime meridian as a **red** line. Color the lines of latitude **yellow**, and the lines of longitude **green.**

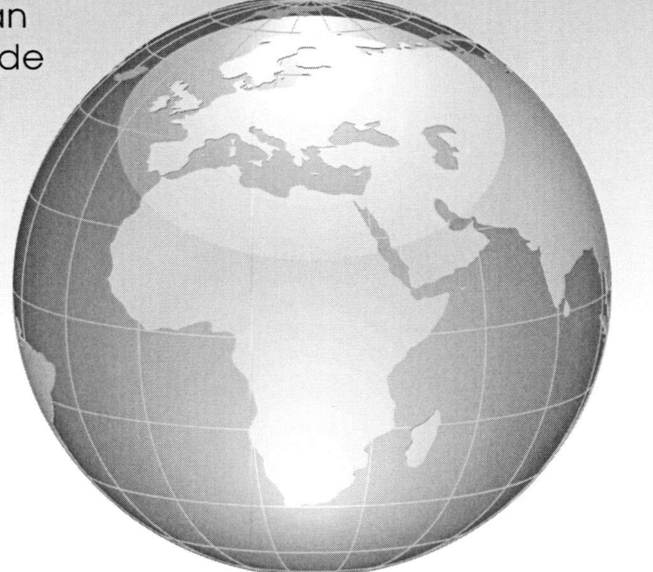

NAME: ____________________

Europe - Location

Describing Europe's **location** can be done in two ways. If we describe Europe's **absolute location**, we are describing exactly where it is found. When we describe Europe's **relative location**, we describe the things around it and the things that connect it to other places.

A continent like Europe is very large, so it is difficult to give its absolute location. We describe a place's absolute location by looking at where lines of **latitude** and **longitude** cross. If we tried to give the absolute location of Europe, we could only give the location of its farthest boundaries, and some of those boundaries are thousands of miles apart! It is easier to describe Europe's location by looking at those features and places around it.

Europe is located west of Asia and north of Africa. Several large bodies of water surround Europe, and provide **links** between Europe and the other continents. The Atlantic Ocean lies to the west, the Arctic Ocean to the north, and the Mediterranean Sea to the south. In one way, Europe's relative location is unique. Most of Europe is located in the eastern **hemisphere**, but its western portion is in the western hemisphere. Why is this? The **prime meridian**, the north-south line that divides the world into east and west, passes through Europe.

STOP

Describe Europe's relative location.

____

____

____

Europe has many different **climates**. Countries along the Mediterranean Sea have very warm, moderate climates. People flock to vacation in southern France, Italy, and Greece because of the pleasant climates. Countries in northern Europe have warm summers, but very cold and snowy winters. Skiers enjoy the tall snowy mountains in these cold places. In central Europe, the tall, snowy peaks of the Alps also attract skiers in the colder months.

Europe - Location

1. Put a check mark (✓) next to the answer that is most correct.

a) What kind of climate do countries along the Mediterranean Sea have?

- ◯ **A** a harsh, cold climate
- ◯ **B** extremely hot at all times
- ◯ **C** a warm, moderate climate
- ◯ **D** tropical and humid

b) Where in Europe are people most likely to go skiing?

- ◯ **A** on Mount Olympus, Greece
- ◯ **B** in northern Europe and the Alps
- ◯ **C** on the Prime Meridian
- ◯ **D** in Asia

c) In which hemisphere is most of Europe located?

- ◯ **A** north of Africa
- ◯ **B** the western hemisphere
- ◯ **C** the Arctic
- ◯ **D** the eastern hemisphere

2. Circle T if the statement is true or F if it is false.

T = True
F = False

T F a) Europe has many different climates.

T F b) Southern France does not have a warm, moderate climate.

T F c) Greece is located on the Mediterranean Sea.

T F d) Europe is located north of Asia and west of Africa.

T F e) The prime meridian divides the Earth into eastern and western hemispheres.

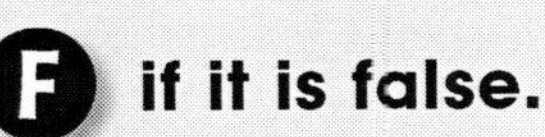

T F f) Relative location tells ***exactly*** where a place is located.

T F g) The Atlantic Ocean lies west of Europe.

After You Read

NAME: ______________________

Europe - Location

Answer the questions in complete sentences.

3. What is the climate of southern Europe? Describe it using examples from the reading.

____

4. Which major bodies of water surround Europe?

____

Research

5. Are these European cities located in the western hemisphere or the eastern hemisphere? Write **W** for the western hemisphere and **E** for the eastern hemisphere in the space beside each city. You may use your atlas to help you.

____ **a) Paris, France**	____ **b) Berlin, Germany**	____ **c) Glasgow, Scotland**
____ **d) Athens, Greece**	____ **e) Bordeaux, France**	____ **f) Rome, Italy**
____ **g) Oslo, Norway**	____ **h) Berne, Switzerland**	____ **i) Moscow, Russia**
____ **j) Warsaw, Poland**	____ **k) Dublin, Ireland**	____ **l) Madrid, Spain**
____ **m) Helsinki, Finland**	____ **n) Florence, Italy**	____ **o) London, England**

6. Find London, England in an atlas, and complete the following activities.

a) What is London's **absolute** location? Give its latitude and longitude.

____

b) What is London's **relative** location? Describe its relative location by describing the things around it.

____

____

7. When a country has no coast on an ocean or a sea, we say that it is **landlocked**. Which European countries are landlocked? List them below. You may use your atlas to help you locate them.

____

____

NAME: ______________________

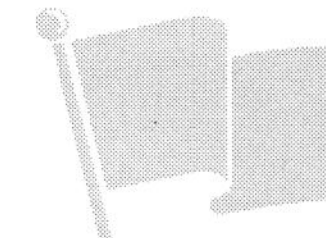

Europe - Place

1. Complete each sentence with a word from the list. Use a dictionary to help you.

a) A [ ] is one of the seven large land masses in the world, each characterized by unique features and human interactions.

b) The art, the music, and the literature of a society are known as its [ ].

c) The animals that live in a particular area are known as that area's [ ].

d) A long, moving body of water, with banks on either side, which flows into another larger body of water, such as an ocean or a lake, is called a [ ].

e) [ ] is a word that describes the way in which a person earns his or her living. A person earns money at work in order to pay for food, shelter, and clothing.

f) A [ ] is a large field where grapes are grown. Grapes grow on a vine.

2. Make a list of those things that make your school unique. Use the chart and the headings to record your ideas.

The look of the school (color, hills, playgrounds)	Plants and animals seen around the school	What is found near the school? (homes, stores, etc.)

Reading Passage

NAME: ____________________

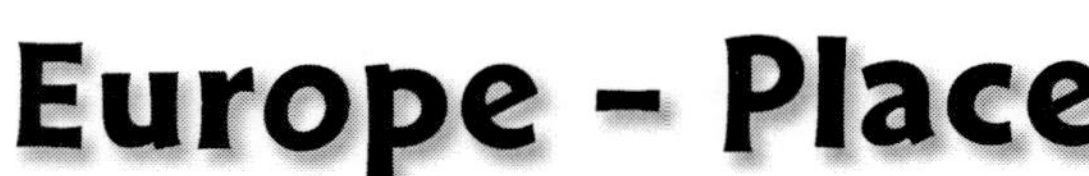

Europe - Place

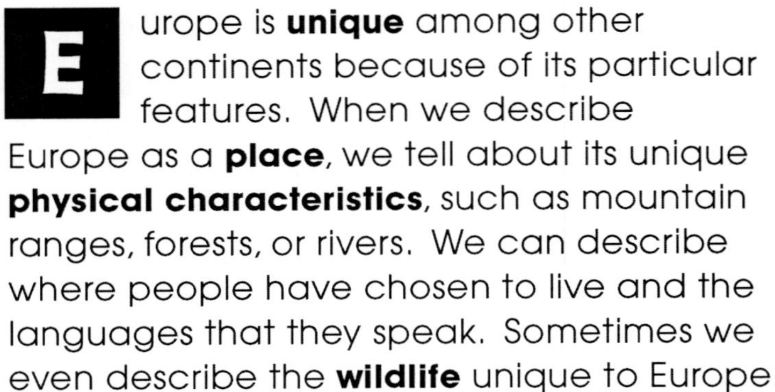

Europe is **unique** among other continents because of its particular features. When we describe Europe as a **place**, we tell about its unique **physical characteristics**, such as mountain ranges, forests, or rivers. We can describe where people have chosen to live and the languages that they speak. Sometimes we even describe the **wildlife** unique to Europe.

Compared to other **continents**, Europe is rather small. However, it is a place made up of more than 40 countries, some large, some small, and more than 720 million people! Many people in Europe live near rivers, seas, or oceans. Some countries in Europe are islands! Many people rely on the sea for food, travel, and their **livelihood**.

Europe has many interesting physical characteristics. Huge forests, unusual cliffs, tall mountain ranges, and deep river valleys are found throughout Europe. The Black Forest is found in southern Germany. The white cliffs of Dover are found on England's eastern **coast**. In central Europe, the Alps tower tall and snow-capped. In France, the Loire River passes through a region of green, fertile lands and vineyards.

There are many important **rivers** in Europe, and many of Europe's largest cities are found on these rivers. The River Thames flows through London to the English Channel. The Seine flows through Paris. Vienna and Budapest, hundreds of miles apart and in different countries, are both found on the Danube River. And on the Tiber, with its long and exciting history, we find Rome, the capital city of Italy. All of these famous cities became important centers of **culture** because their location allowed for travel and **trade**.

STOP

Why are rivers and oceans important for so many Europeans?

____

____

____

NAME: ______________________________

Europe - Place

1. Fill in each blank with a word from the list.

culture	livelihood	largest	rivers	trade
physical characteristics		vineyards	place	

When we describe Europe as a ____________ (a), we can do so in many ways. We can look at its ____________ (b), such as forests, mountains and ____________ (c). An example of a physical characteristic would be the ____________ (d) found in the Loire River Region. Some of Europe's ____________ (e) cities are found on important rivers. They became centers of ____________ (f) and ____________ (g) because of their location. Many people in Europe rely on the sea for their ____________ (h). They fish and travel on the sea.

2. Put a check mark (✓) next to the answer that is most correct.

a) Where is the Black Forest located?

- ◯ **A** in southern Germany
- ◯ **B** in England
- ◯ **C** in France
- ◯ **D** in Budapest

b) Which country does the Tiber wind through?

- ◯ **A** England
- ◯ **B** Germany
- ◯ **C** Rome
- ◯ **D** Italy

c) What are the physical characteristics of the Loire River valley?

- ◯ **A** dry and arid
- ◯ **B** mountainous
- ◯ **C** a humid rainforest
- ◯ **D** green, fertile lands

After You Read

NAME: ______________________________

Europe - Place

Answer each question with a complete sentence.

3. What are some of the physical characteristics of Europe?

____

____

4. Why did some European cities become centers of culture and trade?

____

____

Research

5. Find out more about **one** of these famous European rivers by conducting some simple research. Answer the following questions when conducting your research, and record your findings on a separate piece of paper.

Thames **Rhine** **Rhone** **Tiber** **Seine** **Danube** **Elbe**

- How long is this river?
- Which countries does it pass through?
- Into which large body of water does it flow?
- Which famous cities are located on the river?

6. Because there are so many countries in Europe, many very close to one another, people often speak several different languages to get along with each other. Choose **three** different European countries, and list the various languages spoken there. Make a chart like the example.

Country Name	**Languages Spoken** (i.e., official language(s), and others spoken)

7. Like other continents, Europe has many **endangered species**. Research some of the endangered species of Europe by finding out **how** endangered it is and **why**, and its habitat. Record your information in the chart on the next page. The first species has been given for you.

NAME: ______________________________

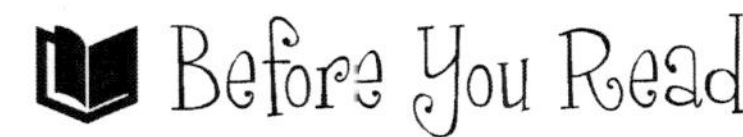

Endangered Species of Europe

Animal Species NAME	HOW Endangered Is It? WHY Is It Endangered?	It's HABITAT
Iberian lynx		

NAME: ______________________

Human/Environment Interactions

1. Complete each sentence with a word from the list. Use a dictionary to help you.

natural resources	environment	positive	interaction	conserve

a) The word ____________________ describes all that surrounds us: the living things around us, the climate, the air we breathe, the water we drink, and the land we live on.

b) ______________________________ are those things that a country possesses that help it function. Examples are oil, water, minerals, and forests. These things are often sold to other countries.

c) ____________________ means to save or to preserve something, such as fuel or a natural resource like water or trees.

d) ____________________ means something that is good, helpful, or constructive.

e) The way one thing acts on another is called an ____________________.

2. Read each of the examples below, and write a sentence describing how it helps preserve our environment.

a) Taking public transportation (i.e., the bus, a train, the subway) to work or school rather than driving your car

____

b) Turning out the lights when you are not using them

____

c) Throwing garbage into garbage cans

____

d) Recycling

____

NAME: ______________________________

Human/Environment Interactions

Every day, the things that people do affect their **environment**. People drive to work on roads that cross lands that were once forests. We work to protect endangered species. Sometimes we build new houses on land that was once farmland. Sometimes we harm the habitats of animals with pollution. Learning about these issues is known as the study of human/environment **interactions**.

In Europe, the **population** is very large for a continent of its size. Cities are crowded and the streets are narrow. There is a great need for **natural resources** and space for the population. Plans are made daily to balance the needs of humans and the environment. Decisions are made about where new housing should be built or about how to control pollution. In London, England, motorists must pay a toll to enter the downtown part of the city to help limit traffic jams and air pollution. In other countries, people try to **conserve** energy, save fuel, and **recycle**, to help protect the natural environment. These are all **positive** human/environment interactions. Unfortunately, sometimes the things we do cause great harm to the environment.

In Europe, people rely on different sources of power to heat their homes and power their vehicles. In April 1986, an accident occurred that caused a **negative** interaction with the environment. The Chernobyl nuclear plant in the Ukraine was used to generate electricity, but an explosion released deadly **radiation** in a cloud that spread across Europe. Workers managed to encase the plant in concrete to stop more radiation from escaping, but many died in the process. Thousands of people had to flee their homes, and people continue to die from the effects of the radiation that was released more than twenty years ago. To this day, it is too dangerous to return to the towns near the nuclear plant.

Why was the accident at Chernobyl a negative human/environment interaction?

____

____

After You Read

NAME: ______________________________

Human/Environment Interactions

1. Complete the chart by putting a check mark in the correct column. Think about what you have read about positive and negative human/environment interactions when deciding where to put your check mark.

Human Action	Positive Interaction	Negative Interaction
a) Cutting down forests for roads		
b) Conserving energy		
c) Protecting endangered species		
d) Recycling		
e) Paying tolls to limit traffic jams and pollution		
f) Building homes on farmland		

2. Circle T if the statement is true or  **if it is false.**

T = True
F = False

T F a) A cloud of deadly radiation from Chernobyl spread over Europe.

T F b) Pollution has a positive affect on animal habitats.

T F c) Many people recycle to protect the natural environment.

T F d) Europe's population is very small for its size.

T F e) European cities are not crowded.

NAME: ______________________________

Human/Environment Interactions

Answer each question with a complete sentence.

3. How did the accident at Chernobyl have a negative affect on the environment? Use examples from the reading in your answer.

____

4. What kinds of actions can people take to help protect the environment as we interact with it?

____

Research, Extensions and Applications

5. What kinds of programs does your school, town, or city have that were chosen because they help protect the environment? Circle which you will be researching.

my school **my neighborhood** **my town** **my city**

Complete a chart like the one below to help you collect your information.

My ______________'s Programs	How they help protect the environment

When you have finished, **create a brochure** showing all the programs in your chosen area. Share the brochure with your class.

6. What things can you do at home to help better protect the environment? List them below.

____

7. Many agencies have been created to help protect the wildlife around us. Here are just a few:

World Wildlife Fund (WWF) **Ducks Unlimited**

The American Society for the Prevention of Cruelty Against Animals (ASPCA)

Research **one** of these agencies. Find out what it does to help protect animals from harm. Share your findings with your class.

NAME: ____________________

Europe - Movement

1. Match the word on the left to its definition on the right. You may use an atlas or a dictionary to help.

1	railway	A network of communication that links one computer to millions of others, and to millions of websites. Ideas and information can be exchanged, and products can be purchased online.	A
2	communication	A means of transportation where trains travel on metal tracks, carrying both people and products. A railway connects places.	B
3	transportation	A person who studies geography, by looking at the physical features of the Earth, the places in which people live, their activities, and the ways in which the earth is changing.	C
4	Internet	The sharing of ideas through many different ways, such as through speech, printed words, signals, sign language, and images.	D
5	geographer	The word used to describe how humans move themselves and other items from place to place. It includes the vehicles we use and the things they travel on (air, water, roads, etc.).	E

2. List at least two ways that the following people or products could be transported between cities, countries, or continents.

automobiles ____________________ ____________________

bananas ____________________ ____________________

travelers ____________________ ____________________

computers ____________________ ____________________

NAME: ______________________________

Europe – Movement

Geographers don't just study what the Earth looks like. They also study what people do each day in different parts of the world. They notice that people travel to work, to school, or to **recreational** activities. Vehicles travel within and between countries and continents delivering the **products** that people use in their homes. People make telephone calls, write letters, watch TV, and surf the Internet looking for information. What do these things all have in common? They all involve **movement**, the word geographers use to describe how people, ideas, and products move from place to place.

Transportation is the word we use to describe movement involving vehicles. In Europe, people have long relied on trains to help them get from place to place. **Railways** are also used to deliver the products Europeans use daily, such as food, furniture, electronics, and fuel. One of the most important places in any European city is the train station. Roads and **highways** are everywhere. Bicycles, cars, motorcycles, motor scooters, buses, and trucks are used each day. European streets are much narrower than those in North America, so small cars are preferred over large ones. People in Europe also travel by plane or by ship. Many products are delivered along rivers and **canals**, avoiding the traffic jams that can happen on highways. Did you know that the city of Venice, Italy, is famous for its canals? People must travel from place to place by gondola!

STOP

On which forms of transportation do Europeans rely?

____

____

____

Communication also plays an important part in movement. Ideas can be carried from place to place by radio, television, the **Internet**, letters, telephones, or even by visiting the local coffee shop to chat with friends. Europe also has many hundreds of newspapers to help spread the news and opinions.

NAME: ___________________________

Europe – Movement

1. Circle T if the statement is true or F if it is false.

T = True
F = False

T F a) Geographers study the Earth and what people do in different parts of the world.

T F b) Transportation is a word we use to describe movement involving vehicles.

T F c) Florence is famous for its canals.

T F d) People do not rely on trains in Europe for travel and to deliver products from place to place.

T F e) Europe has many newspapers to help spread news and opinions.

T F f) Europeans rely only on the telephone and letter writing for communication.

2. Match the word on the left to its meaning on the right.

	Word	Meaning	
1	movement	A word used to describe the passing of information or ideas from one person to another, or to a group, using devices such as radios, television, a telephone, or the Internet, or simply through a discussion	A
2	transportation	Movement involving vehicles	B
3	communication	A large building where trains stop to pick up, or to drop off passengers or products	C
4	train station	A word used to describe how people, ideas, and products move from place to place	D
5	recreational activities	The free-time activities people do to relax and enjoy themselves after their work is done	E

NAME: ______________________________

Europe - Movement

Answer each question with a complete sentence.

3. In what different ways do people communicate their ideas?

____

4. Trains are very important in Europe. Have you ever been on a train? If yes, describe where you were going, and what the train was like.

____

Research and Extensions

5. Look at the transportation map of Europe & research rail travel in Europe on the web.

When collecting your facts, think of these points:

- Which countries rely heavily on road travel?
- Where are some famous train stations located?
- Is rail travel more expensive than driving? Which is faster?

Share your findings with the class in the form of a **short essay**. Use each question as the topic for a paragraph.

6. River travel is also important in Europe. One river, in particular, is famous for its cruises that tourists from around the world flock to take. That river is the Rhine. It flows through several European countries.

Research Rhine River cruises. If you took this cruise, what would you see? What interesting things are there for tourists to do? Present your findings as a pamphlet or a poster advertising what you have learned. Illustrate your work. Share your findings with the class.

7. While your family may have lived in your current home for a number of years, your extended family and ancestors probably came from a variety of different places, in a variety of different ways. **Interview** your parents to find out where your family **originated**. Find out how and when they moved about, and how and when your immediate family came to live in your present home. Record your findings and share them with your class.

NAME: ____________________

Europe - Regions

1. Match the word on the left to its definition on the right. You may use an atlas or a dictionary to help.

1	**peninsula**	The features of a place that help us recognize and describe it. They may include mountains, valleys, plains, forests, deserts, or bodies of water.	A
2	**climate**	A long area of land that is surrounded by water on both sides and at its tip. It is connected to the mainland at one end, stretching out from the mainland like a finger.	B
3	**vegetation**	The weather conditions of an area, including winds, temperature, and precipitation.	C
4	**physical characteristics**	The plants that grow in a particular place.	D

2. Compare the following rooms in your school using the Venn diagram. How are they the same? How are they different?

my classroom

the gym

the library

NAME: ____________________

Europe – Regions

Geographers use the word **region** to describe an area of land. A region can be either small or large, and can be studied over time to see how it changes. A region is described by the **features** that make it **unique**. Geographers look at a region's **physical characteristics**, such as mountain ranges or **vegetation**, to see how it is different from others. Another way to describe a region is by **language**, or by looking at where, how, and why people live in a certain area. Europe has a wide variety of regions.

Provence is in southeastern France at the southern part of the Alps. It is a hilly region that borders on the Mediterranean Sea. It is known for its warm **climate** and beautiful scenery. Ancient Roman ruins can be found in Provence. The bridges in the town of Avignon are famous in song. Artists have painted its fields of **lavender** and sunflowers, and stories have been written about the small villages found throughout the hills. However, when the dry and cold **mistral** winds blow, people find shelter and enjoy the food and drink for which the region is famous.

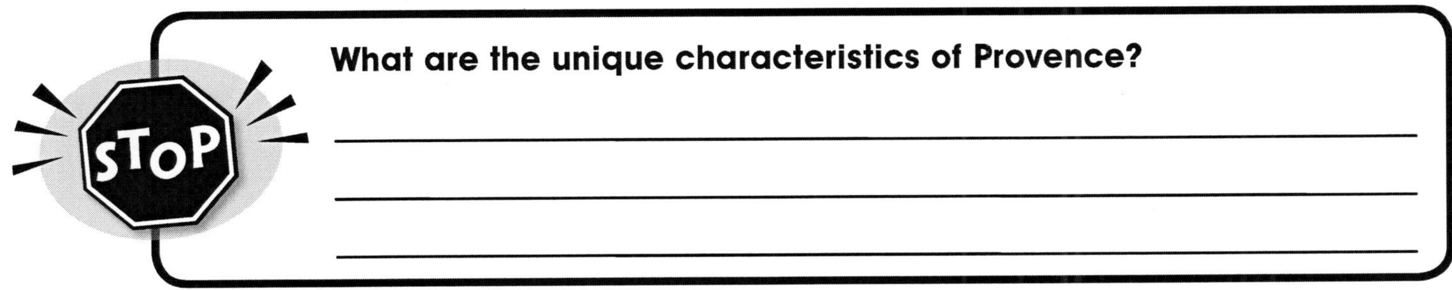

What are the unique characteristics of Provence?

____

____

____

The Peloponnese is a region found in southern Greece. It is a **peninsula** separated from the rest of Greece by a deep canal at Corinth. The region is hilly, with twisty mountain roads. Small villages dot the landscape, with many older homes left vacant as young people moved to the cities. Winter days are mild, with cold nights, but summer days are very hot. Driving through the Peloponnese, you might see sheep, apple orchards, and people making cheese. One specialty of the region is green Kalamata olives, famous for their taste.

After You Read

NAME: ______________________________

Europe – Regions

1. Match the region to each of its features using arrows. The first has been done for you.

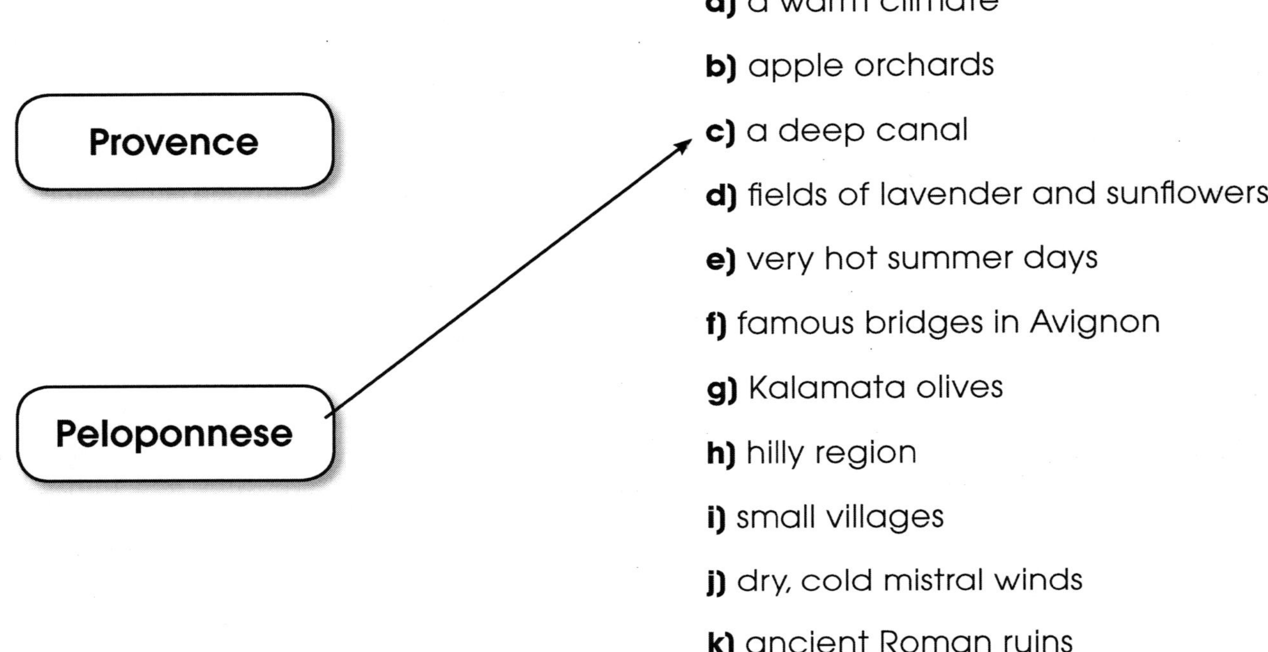

a) a warm climate

b) apple orchards

c) a deep canal

d) fields of lavender and sunflowers

e) very hot summer days

f) famous bridges in Avignon

g) Kalamata olives

h) hilly region

i) small villages

j) dry, cold mistral winds

k) ancient Roman ruins

2. Put a check mark (✓) next to the answer that is most correct.

a) Why are some homes in the Peloponnese empty?

- ○ **A** they are old and unsafe
- ○ **B** younger people have left them behind and moved away to the cities
- ○ **C** people prefer newer homes
- ○ **D** prices are high

b) Which human activities and features are studied when geographers look at a region?

- ○ **A** the language(s) spoken
- ○ **B** where people live
- ○ **C** why people live where they do
- ○ **D** all of the above

NAME: ______________________________

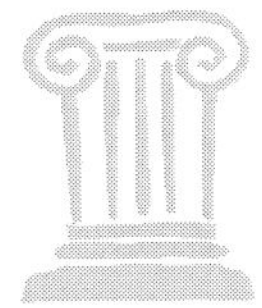

Europe - Regions

Answer each question with a complete sentence.

3. Which features are used to describe a region?

____

____

4. What features make the Peloponnese unique?

____

____

Research and Extensions

5. Compare **two** different regions in Europe using the Venn diagram on the next page. You will need to conduct some simple research to find facts to include in your Venn diagram.

When collecting information, try to find answers to these questions:

- What are the physical characteristics that make each region unique?
- What kinds of human activities take place there? Where do people live in these regions?
- What language or languages are spoken there?
- What vegetation grows in these areas?

Find answers to these questions for **two** of the following regions:

Provence | **the Peloponnese** | **the Black Forest** | **the Russian steppes**

The Scottish highlands | **the Pyrenees mountains** | **the Loire River region**

After You Read

NAME: ____________________

Venn Diagram

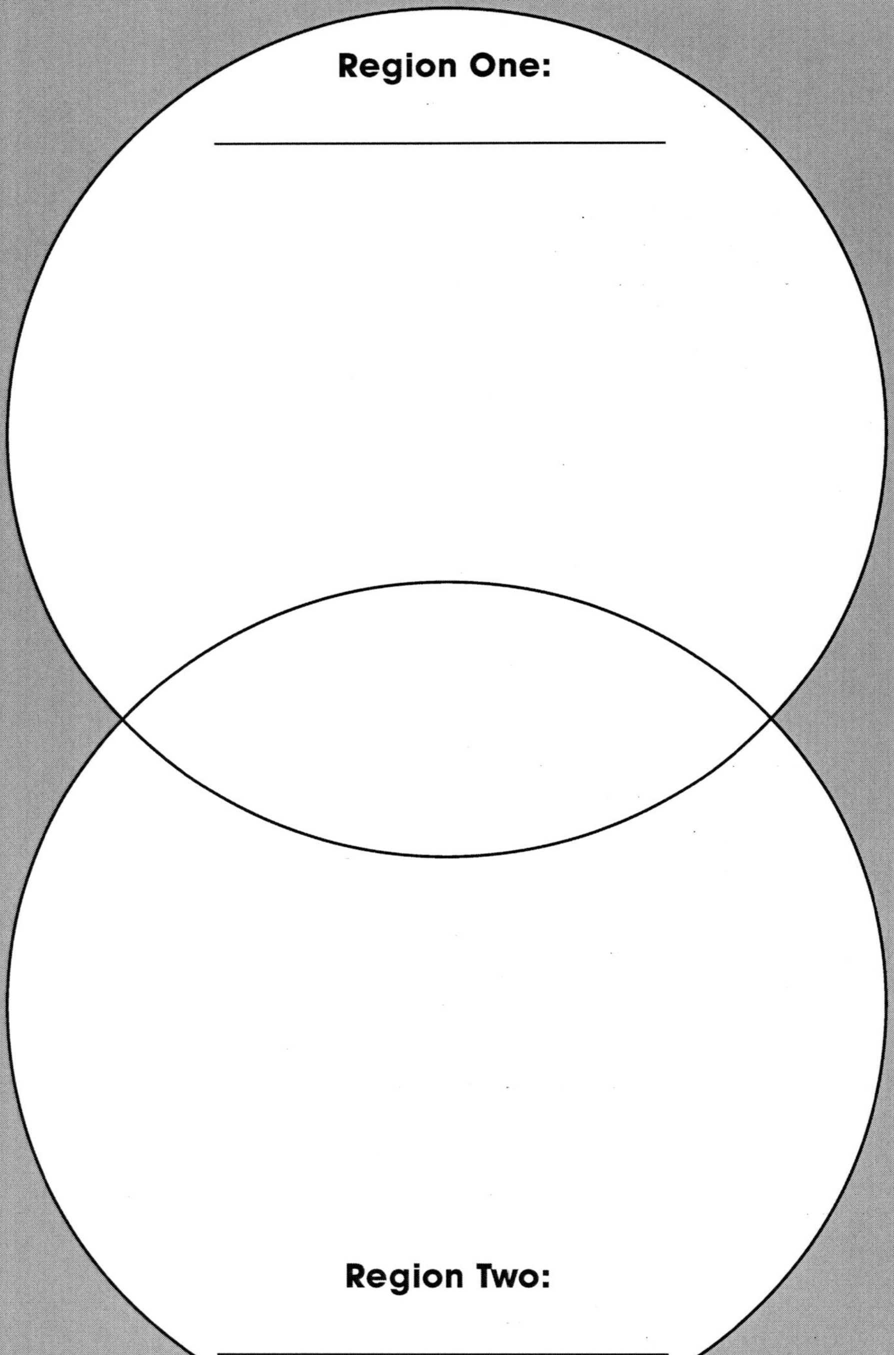

Region One:

____

Region Two:

____

NAME: ______________________________

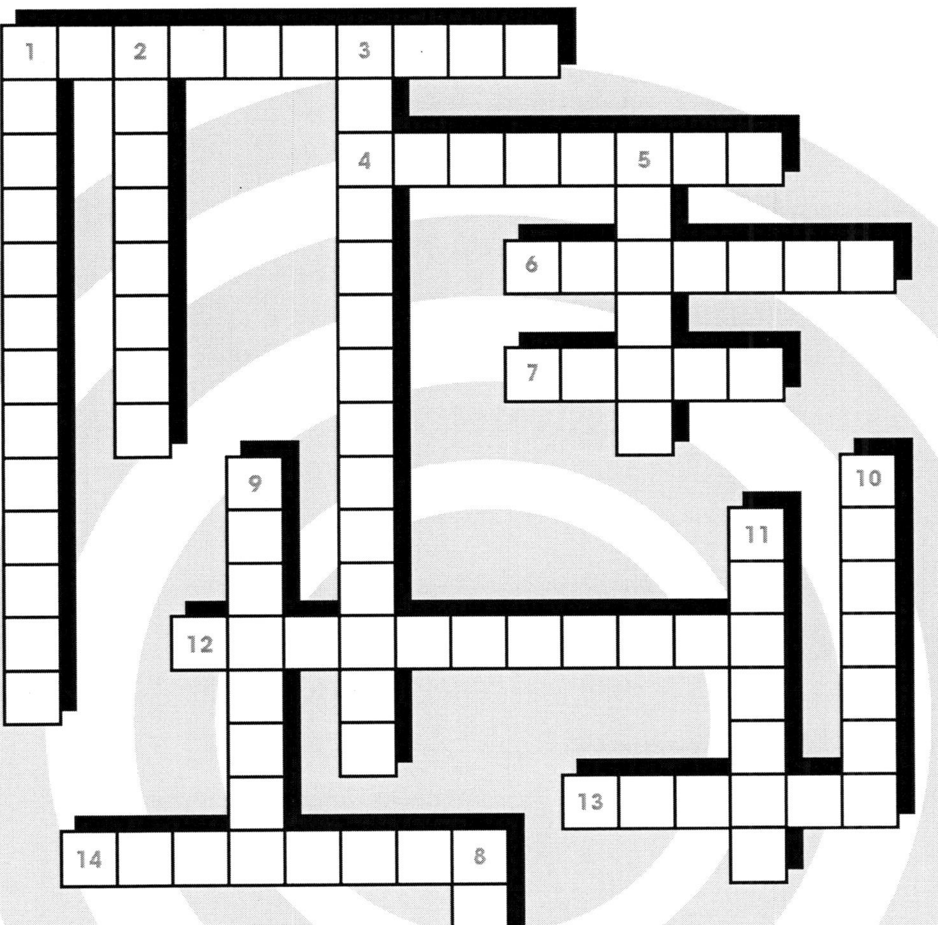

Word List

- physical
- vineyard
- unique
- population
- islands
- hemispheres
- south
- absolute
- prime meridian
- canals
- transportation
- products
- mistral
- climate
- route

Across

1 Europe's _____ is very large for its size

4 _____ location descibes exactly where a place is

6 The temperature, rain and/or snowfall found in a place

7 A path taken from one place to another

12 Europe is found in the east and west ____

13 Many products are transported along ______

14 Things people use at home, work and school

Down

1 The _____ divides the world into east and west

2 A place can be described by ____ and human characteristics

3 Movement involving vehicles

5 A region is described by its ____ features

8 The Mediterranean Sea lies to the _____ of Europe

9 Large field where grapes are grown

10 Some countries in Europe are ____

11 Provence, France is know for its cold ____ winds

NAME: 

Word Search

Find all of the words in the Word Search. Words may be horizontal, vertical, or diagonal. A few may even be backwards! Look carefully!

hemisphere	nuclear	trade	features
boundaries	lavender	interaction	livelihood
landlocked	peninsula	conserve	culture
vineyard	location	railway	European
travel	climate	Internet	Italy
environment	continent	villages	river
resources	coast	prime meridian	olives

b	o	u	n	d	a	r	i	e	s	a	l	p	c	q	e	w	p
e	l	r	t	y	u	t	r	a	d	e	i	e	o	u	u	i	r
n	a	o	c	r	a	i	l	w	a	y	v	n	a	p	r	p	i
u	n	i	a	l	s	d	f	g	h	j	e	i	s	e	o	j	m
c	d	n	h	j	i	k	l	b	s	v	l	n	t	r	p	d	e
l	l	t	z	x	c	m	v	b	e	n	i	s	m	u	e	r	m
e	o	e	a	m	n	b	a	v	a	c	h	u	x	t	a	a	e
a	c	r	a	g	i	h	c	t	b	f	o	l	f	l	n	y	r
r	k	n	f	g	g	o	n	t	e	t	o	a	y	u	y	e	i
m	e	e	g	g	n	e	r	t	r	s	d	s	d	c	d	n	d
e	d	t	r	s	n	e	q	w	e	r	t	y	u	i	o	i	i
h	g	t	e	i	d	a	n	n	s	e	g	a	l	l	i	v	a
e	i	r	t	n	n	n	o	n	t	r	a	v	e	l	n	n	n
y	v	n	e	v	t	i	i	a	n	e	r	t	y	u	i	o	h
e	o	v	n	n	t	n	t	r	e	s	o	u	r	c	e	s	d
c	a	t	g	a	v	b	c	b	m	v	w	e	r	t	y	u	s
l	m	n	c	b	v	c	a	x	n	f	r	t	g	d	e	s	e
p	l	o	j	h	g	f	r	t	o	y	u	e	b	v	c	d	r
u	l	y	t	r	g	b	e	n	r	v	o	c	s	a	n	d	u
p	l	o	k	u	h	t	t	y	i	v	g	h	j	n	i	h	t
l	i	t	a	l	y	t	n	o	v	c	u	p	i	c	o	c	a
a	e	i	o	u	y	a	i	e	n	o	l	i	v	e	s	c	e
h	e	m	i	s	p	h	e	r	e	e	r	i	v	e	r	v	f

NAME: ______________________________

Comprehension Quiz

30

Part A

Circle T if the statement is true or F if it is false.

T = True
F = False

8

T F **a)** Most of Europe is in the eastern hemisphere.

T F **b)** The prime meridian divides the world into eastern and western hemispheres.

T F **c)** The plants that grow in a place are called vegetation.

T F **d)** Provence is a cold, snowy region of France.

T F **e)** The accident at the Chernobyl nuclear plant caused thousands to move away, and caused many illnesses and deaths.

T F **f)** Very few Europeans rely on the sea for their livelihoods.

T F **g)** Latitude and longitude are used to find a place's absolute location.

T F **h)** River and rail travel are very important in Europe.

Part B

Label the map by doing the following:

6

1. Show the following features on the map by writing the letter on the map in the correct location.

a) Europe
b) Asia
c) Africa
d) Atlantic Ocean
e) Mediterranean Sea

2. Color the prime meridian **red**.

SUBTOTAL: /14

After You Read

NAME: ____________________

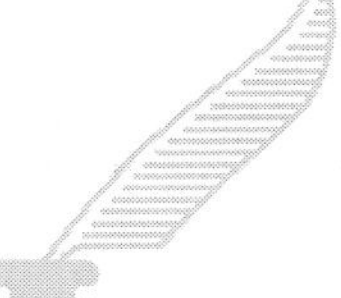

Comprehension Quiz

Part C

Answer the questions in complete sentences.

1. What is the difference between **absolute** location and **relative** location? As an example, describe Europe's relative location. 4

____

____

____

2. How do we describe **place**? Give examples when answering. 3

____

____

3. Describe what is meant by **human and environment interactions**. Explain how recycling is a positive interaction. 3

____

____

4. What do we mean by **movement** in geography? Give one example of transportation and one of communication. 3

____

____

____

5. What is a **region**? How can we describe one? Give a European example. 3

____

____

____

SUBTOTAL: /16

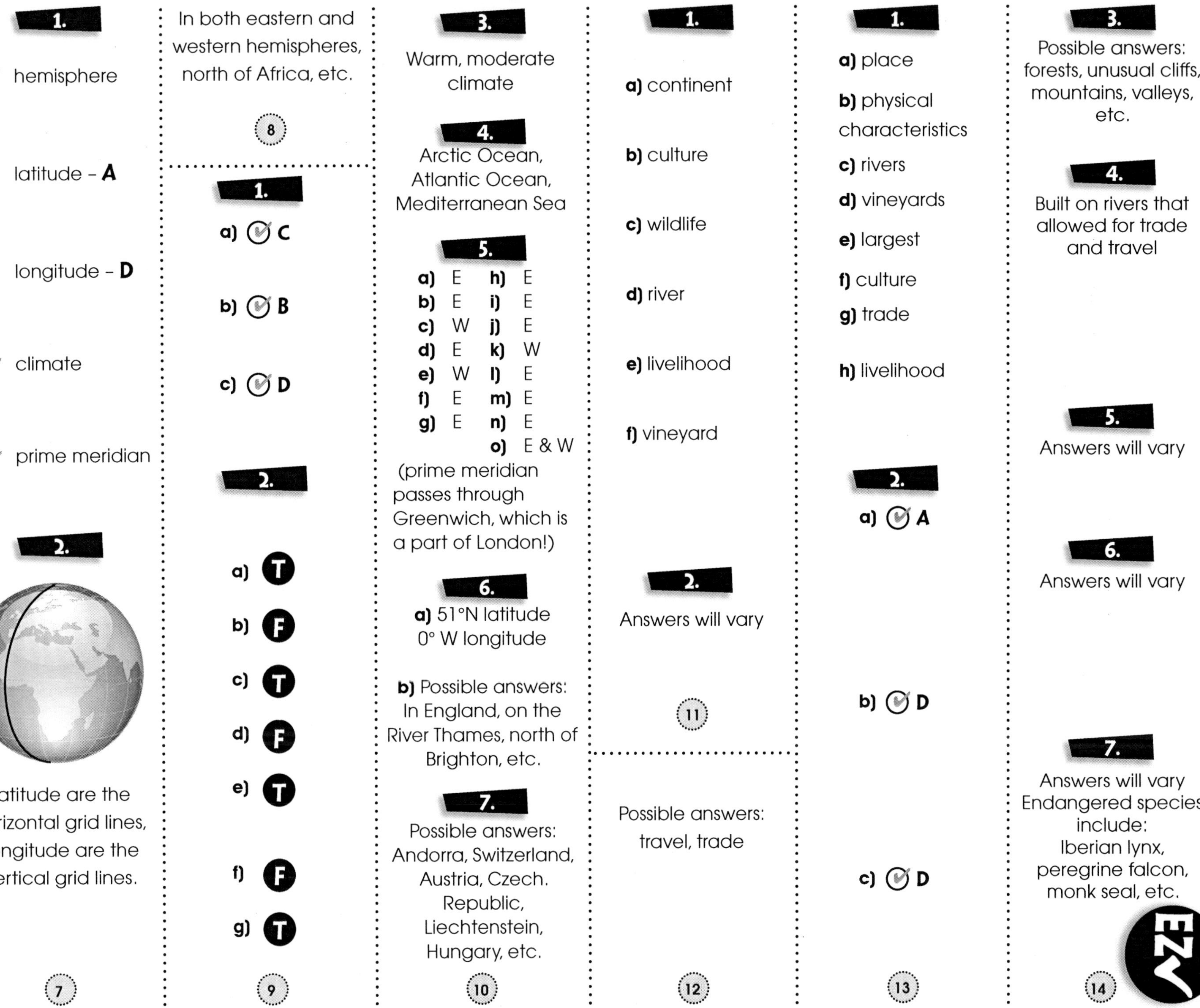

1.

✔ hemisphere

✘ latitude – **A**

✘ longitude – **D**

✔ climate

✔ prime meridian

2.

Latitude are the horizontal grid lines, Longitude are the vertical grid lines.

7

In both eastern and western hemispheres, north of Africa, etc.

8

1.

a) ✔ **C**

b) ✔ **B**

c) ✔ **D**

2.

a) **T**

b) **F**

c) **T**

d) **F**

e) **T**

f) **F**

g) **T**

9

3.

Warm, moderate climate

4.

Arctic Ocean, Atlantic Ocean, Mediterranean Sea

5.

a)	E	**h)**	E
b)	E	**i)**	E
c)	W	**j)**	E
d)	E	**k)**	W
e)	W	**l)**	E
f)	E	**m)**	E
g)	E	**n)**	E
		o)	E & W

(prime meridian passes through Greenwich, which is a part of London!)

6.

a) 51°N latitude 0° W longitude

b) Possible answers: In England, on the River Thames, north of Brighton, etc.

7.

Possible answers: Andorra, Switzerland, Austria, Czech. Republic, Liechtenstein, Hungary, etc.

10

1.

a) continent

b) culture

c) wildlife

d) river

e) livelihood

f) vineyard

2.

Answers will vary

11

Possible answers: travel, trade

12

1.

a) place

b) physical characteristics

c) rivers

d) vineyards

e) largest

f) culture

g) trade

h) livelihood

2.

a) ✔ **A**

b) ✔ **D**

c) ✔ **D**

13

3.

Possible answers: forests, unusual cliffs, mountains, valleys, etc.

4.

Built on rivers that allowed for trade and travel

5.

Answers will vary

6.

Answers will vary

7.

Answers will vary Endangered species include: Iberian lynx, peregrine falcon, monk seal, etc.

14

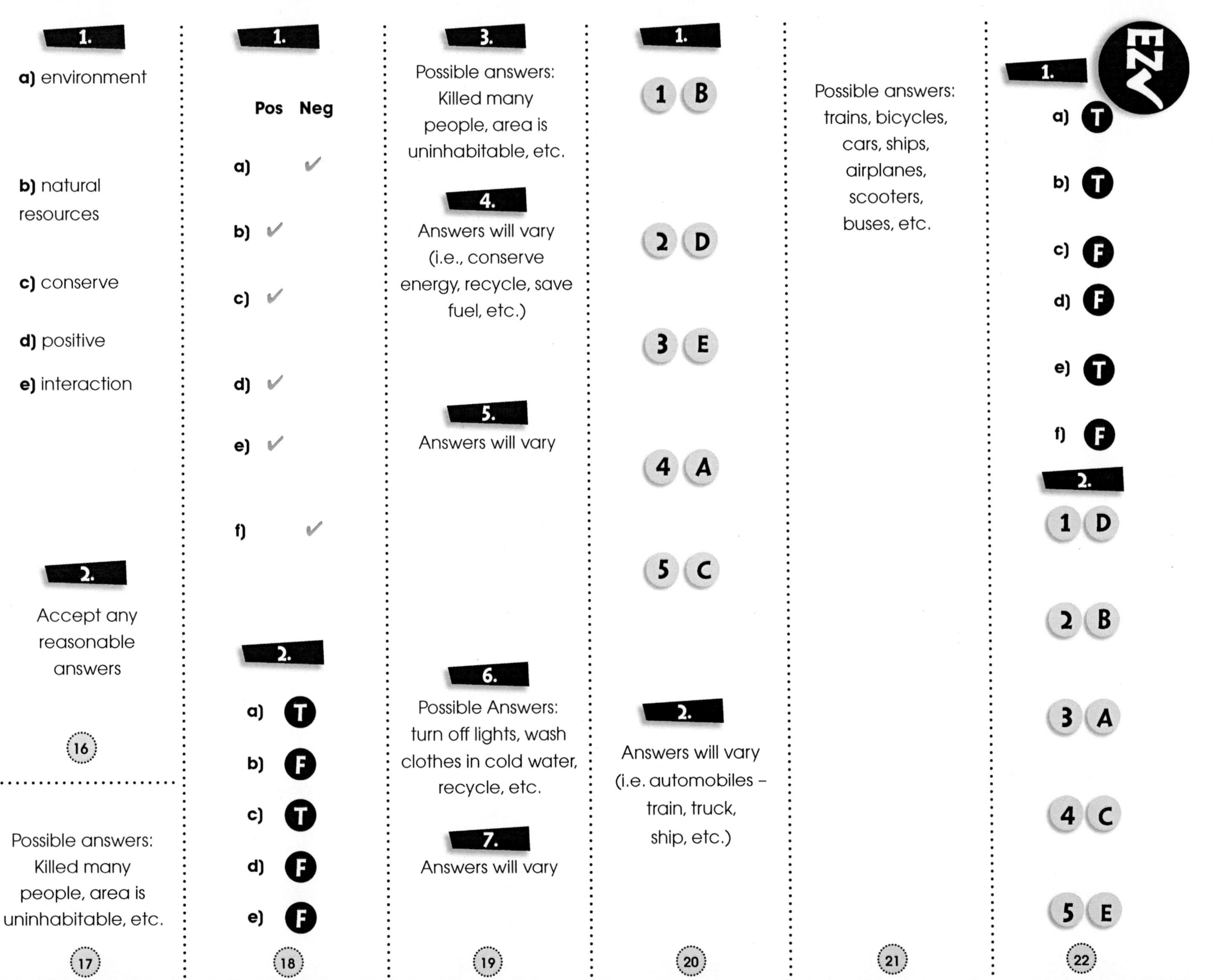

Page 16

1.

a) environment

b) natural resources

c) conserve

d) positive

e) interaction

2.

Accept any reasonable answers

Page 17

Possible answers: Killed many people, area is uninhabitable, etc.

Page 18

1.

	Pos	Neg
a)		✔
b)	✔	
c)	✔	
d)	✔	
e)	✔	
f)		✔

2.

a) T
b) F
c) T
d) F
e) F

Page 19

3.

Possible answers: Killed many people, area is uninhabitable, etc.

4.

Answers will vary (i.e., conserve energy, recycle, save fuel, etc.)

5.

Answers will vary

6.

Possible Answers: turn off lights, wash clothes in cold water, recycle, etc.

7.

Answers will vary

Page 20

1.

1 B
2 D
3 E
4 A
5 C

2.

Answers will vary (i.e. automobiles – train, truck, ship, etc.)

Page 21

Possible answers: trains, bicycles, cars, ships, airplanes, scooters, buses, etc.

Page 22

1.

a) T
b) T
c) F
d) F
e) T
f) F

2.

1 D
2 B
3 A
4 C
5 E

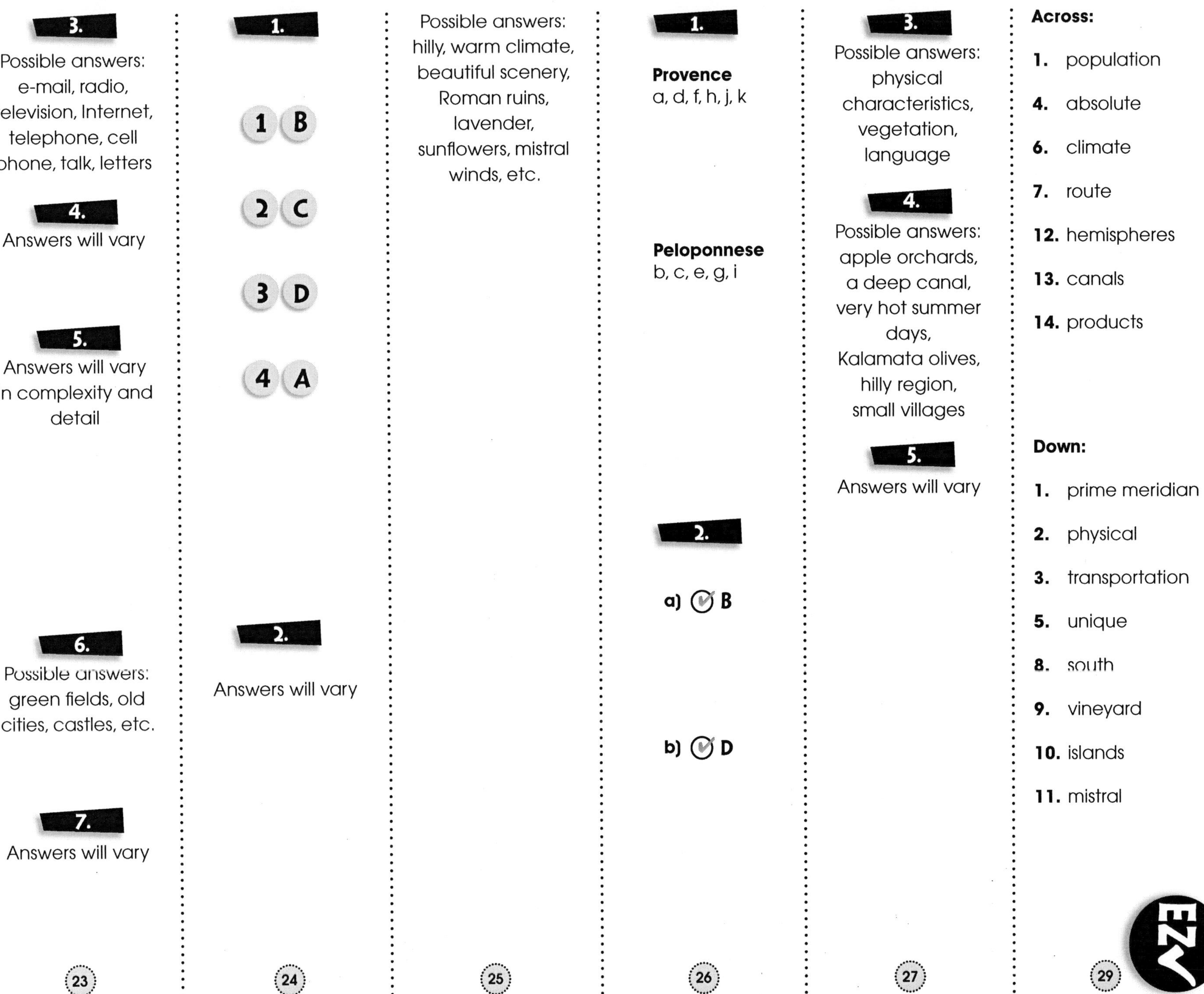

3.
Possible answers: e-mail, radio, television, Internet, telephone, cell phone, talk, letters

4.
Answers will vary

5.
Answers will vary in complexity and detail

6.
Possible answers: green fields, old cities, castles, etc.

7.
Answers will vary

23

1.

1 B

2 C

3 D

4 A

2.
Answers will vary

24

Possible answers: hilly, warm climate, beautiful scenery, Roman ruins, lavender, sunflowers, mistral winds, etc.

25

1.

Provence
a, d, f, h, j, k

Peloponnese
b, c, e, g, i

2.

a) ✓ B

b) ✓ D

26

3.
Possible answers: physical characteristics, vegetation, language

4.
Possible answers: apple orchards, a deep canal, very hot summer days, Kalamata olives, hilly region, small villages

5.
Answers will vary

27

Across:

1. population
4. absolute
6. climate
7. route
12. hemispheres
13. canals
14. products

Down:

1. prime meridian
2. physical
3. transportation
5. unique
8. south
9. vineyard
10. islands
11. mistral

29

EZ✓

Word Search Answers

b	o	u	n	d	a	r	i	e	s	a	l	p	c	q	e	w	p
e	l	r	t	y	u	t	r	a	d	e	i	e	o	u	u	i	r
n	a	o	c	r	a	i	l	w	a	y	v	n	a	p	r	p	i
u	n	i	a	l	s	d	f	g	h	j	e	i	s	e	o	j	m
c	d	n	h	j	i	k	l	b	s	v	l	n	t	r	p	d	e
l	l	t	z	x	c	m	v	b	e	n	i	s	m	u	e	r	m
e	o	e	a	m	n	b	a	v	a	c	h	u	x	t	a	a	e
a	c	r	a	g	i	h	c	t	b	f	o	l	f	l	n	y	r
r	k	n	f	g	g	o	n	t	e	t	o	a	y	u	y	e	i
m	e	e	g	g	n	e	r	t	r	s	d	s	d	c	d	n	d
e	d	t	r	s	n	e	q	w	e	r	t	y	u	i	o	i	i
h	g	t	e	i	d	a	n	n	s	e	g	a	l	l	i	v	a
e	i	r	t	n	n	n	o	n	t	r	a	v	e	l	n	n	n
y	v	n	e	v	t	i	i	a	n	e	r	t	y	u	i	o	h
e	o	v	n	n	t	n	t	r	e	s	o	u	r	c	e	s	d
c	a	t	g	a	v	b	c	b	m	v	w	e	r	t	y	u	s
l	m	n	c	b	v	c	a	x	n	f	r	t	g	d	e	s	e
p	l	o	j	h	g	f	r	t	o	y	u	e	b	v	c	d	r
u	l	y	t	r	g	b	e	n	r	v	o	c	s	a	n	d	u
p	l	o	k	u	h	t	t	y	i	v	g	h	j	n	i	h	t
l	i	t	a	l	y	t	n	o	v	c	u	p	i	c	o	c	a
a	e	i	o	u	y	a	i	e	n	o	l	i	v	e	s	c	e
h	e	m	i	s	p	h	e	r	e	e	r	i	v	e	r	v	f

Part A

a) T

b) T

c) T

d) F

e) T

f) F

g) T

h) T

Part B

1.

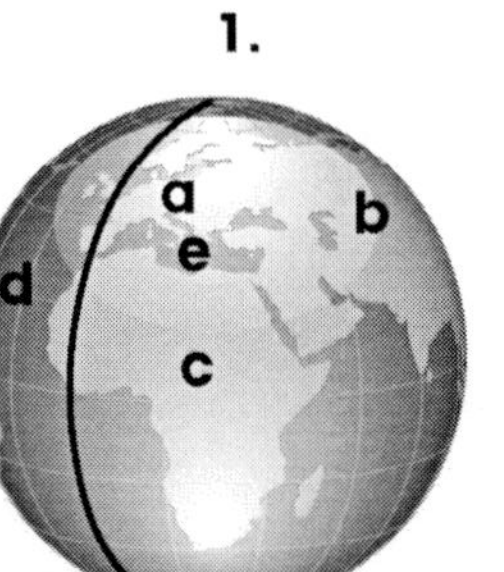

Prime meridian

Part C

1.
Possible answers:
Absolute – gives a place's exact location using latitude and longitude;
Relative – gives a place's location by describing the features around it, and the connections it has to other places;
Europe – north of Africa, west of Asia, east of Atlantic Ocean, north of Mediterranean Sea

2. Possible answers:
Mountains, plains, rivers, towns, cities

3. Possible answers:
How humans and the environment interact, in both positive and negative ways
Recycling – reuses things so we do not litter or create more garbage, preserve resources, etc.

4. Possible answers:
How people, ideas, and products are moved from place to place (i.e., plane, train, ship, bus, bicycle, e-mail, radio, television, Internet, telephone)

5. Possible answers:
Large or small area of land described by its features, physical characteristics, vegetation, language

Europe World Location Map

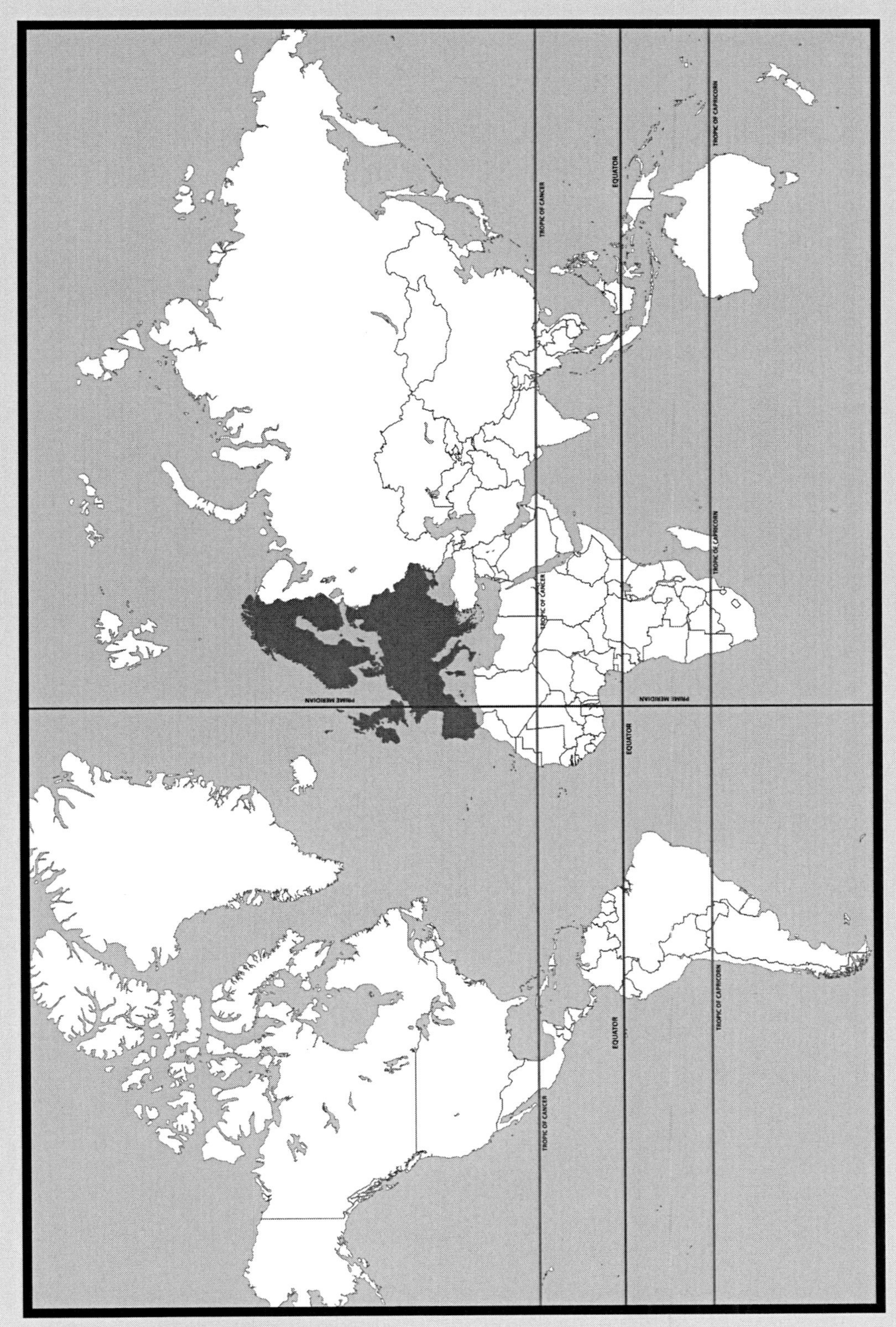

Europe Globe View Map

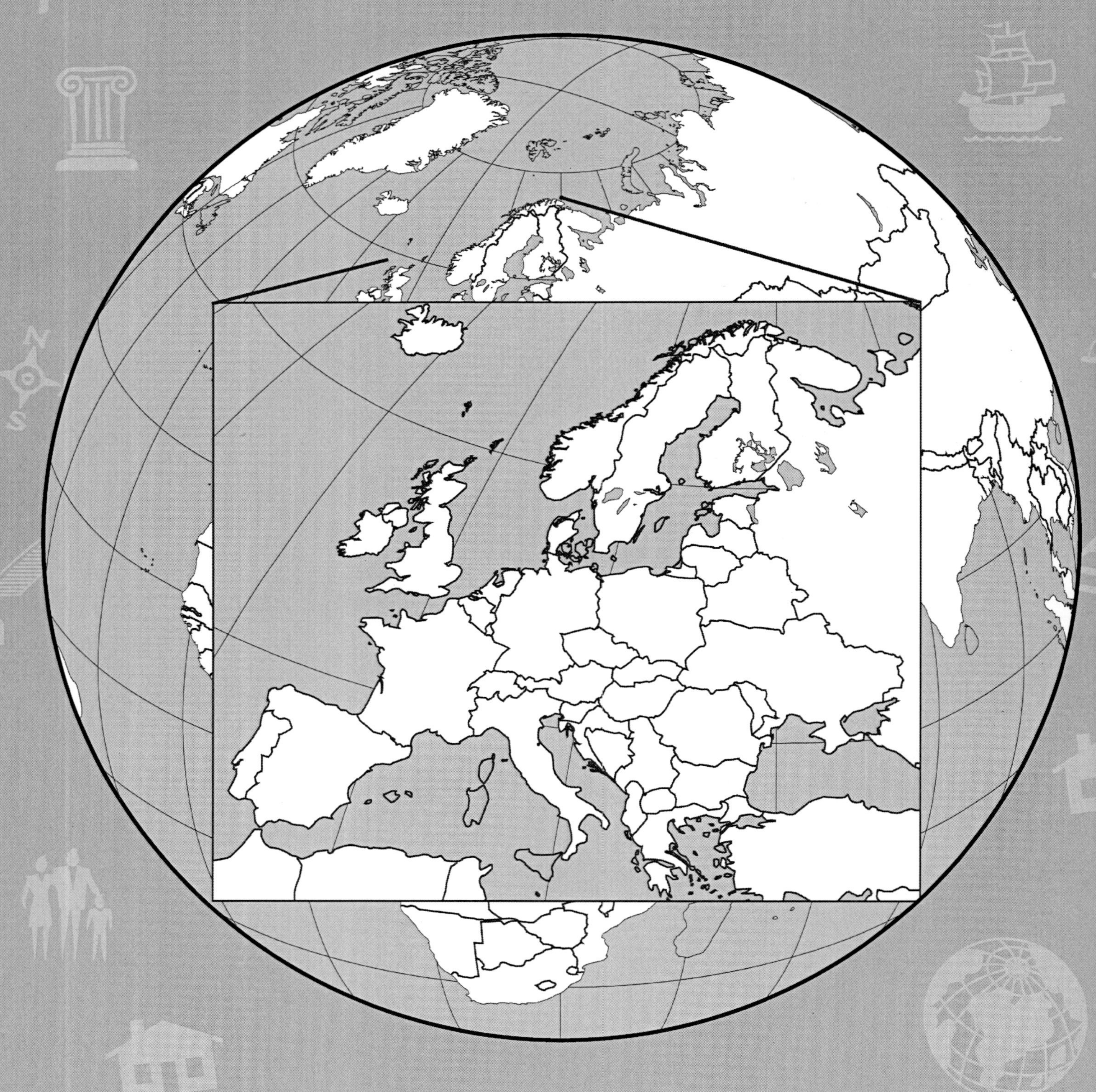

Europe Outline Map

Europe Physical Map

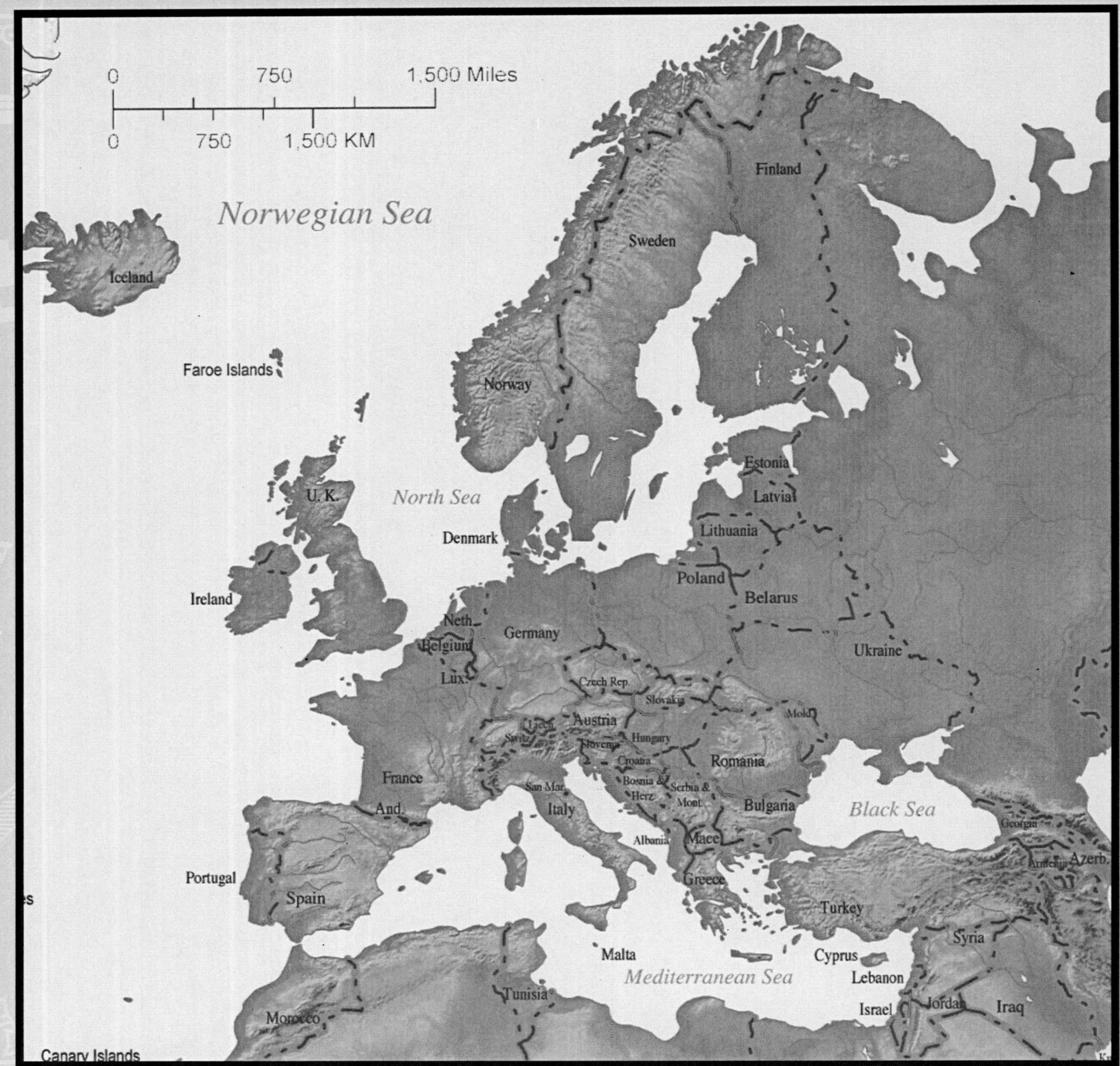

Europe
Major Population Map

Europe Political Map

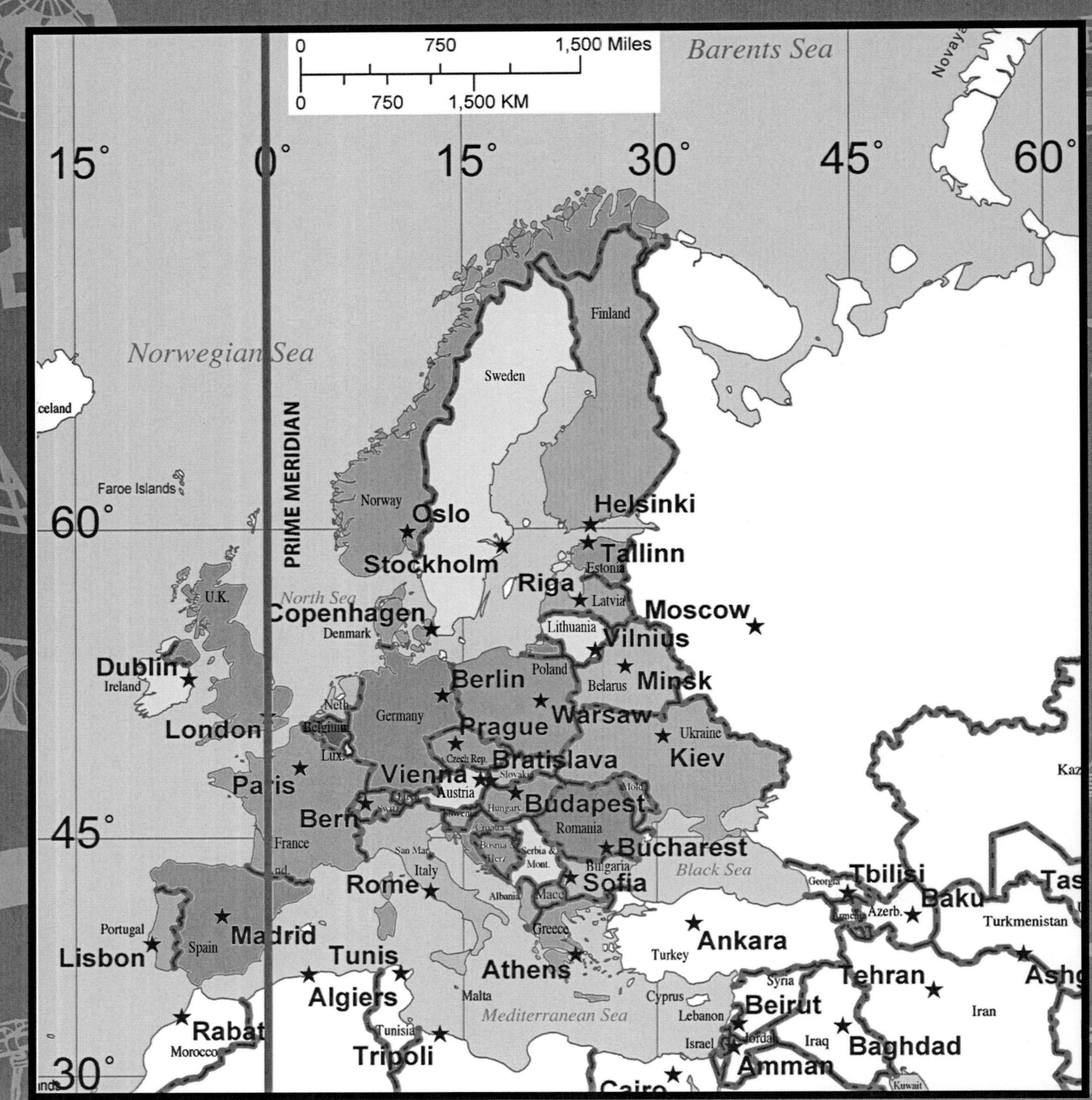

Europe Transportation Map

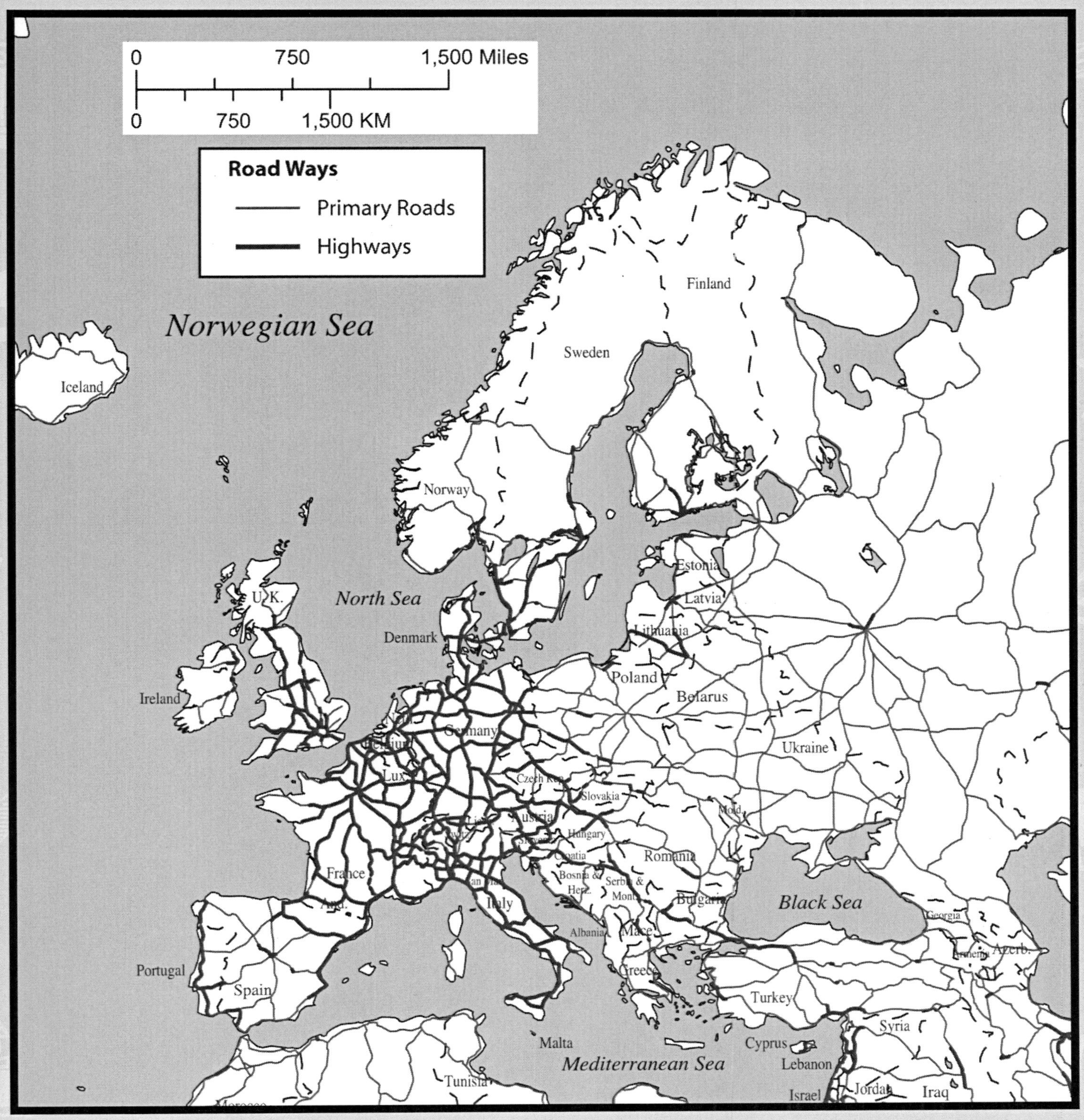

Europe Waterway Map

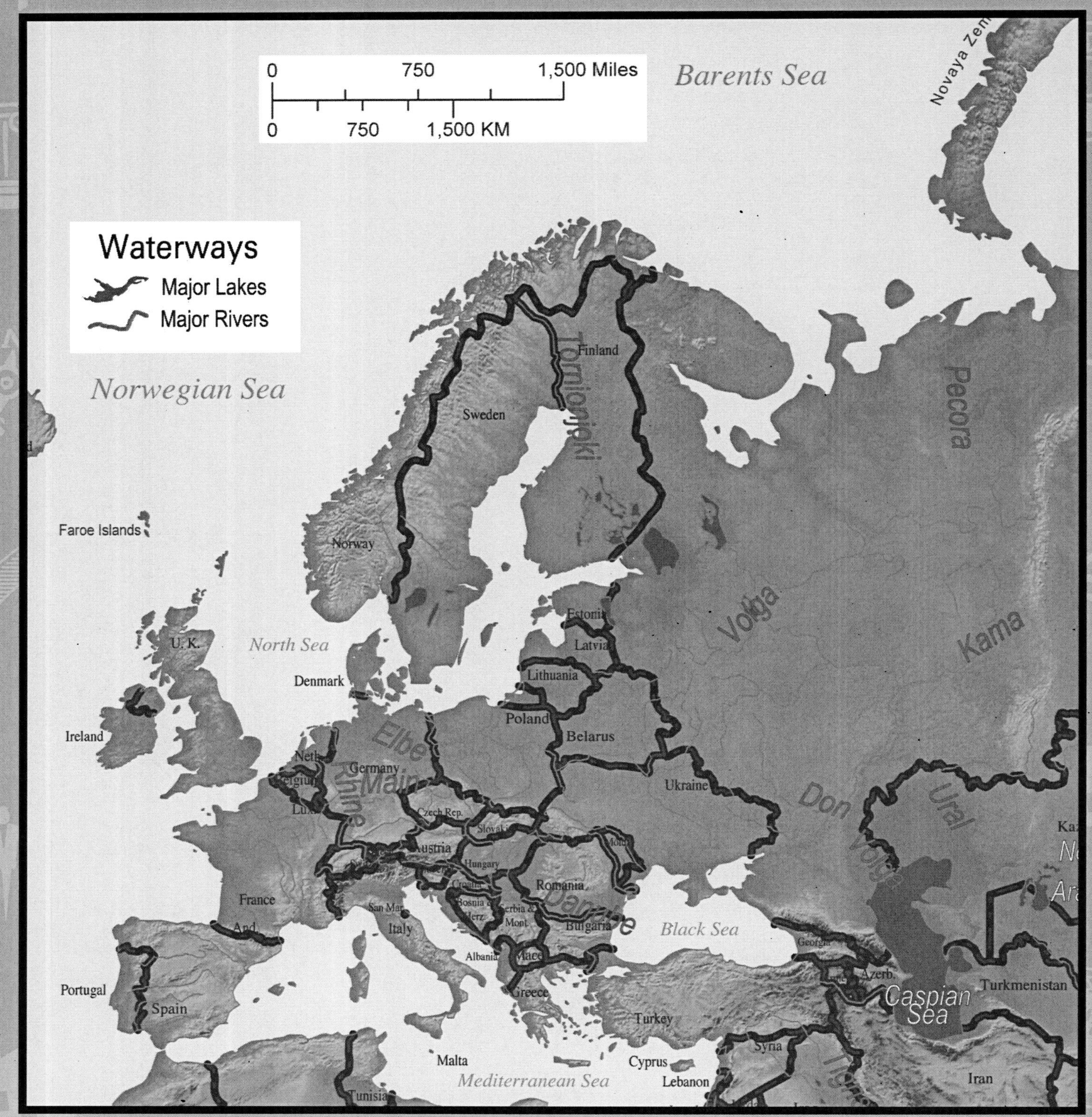

Europe Continent Outline Map

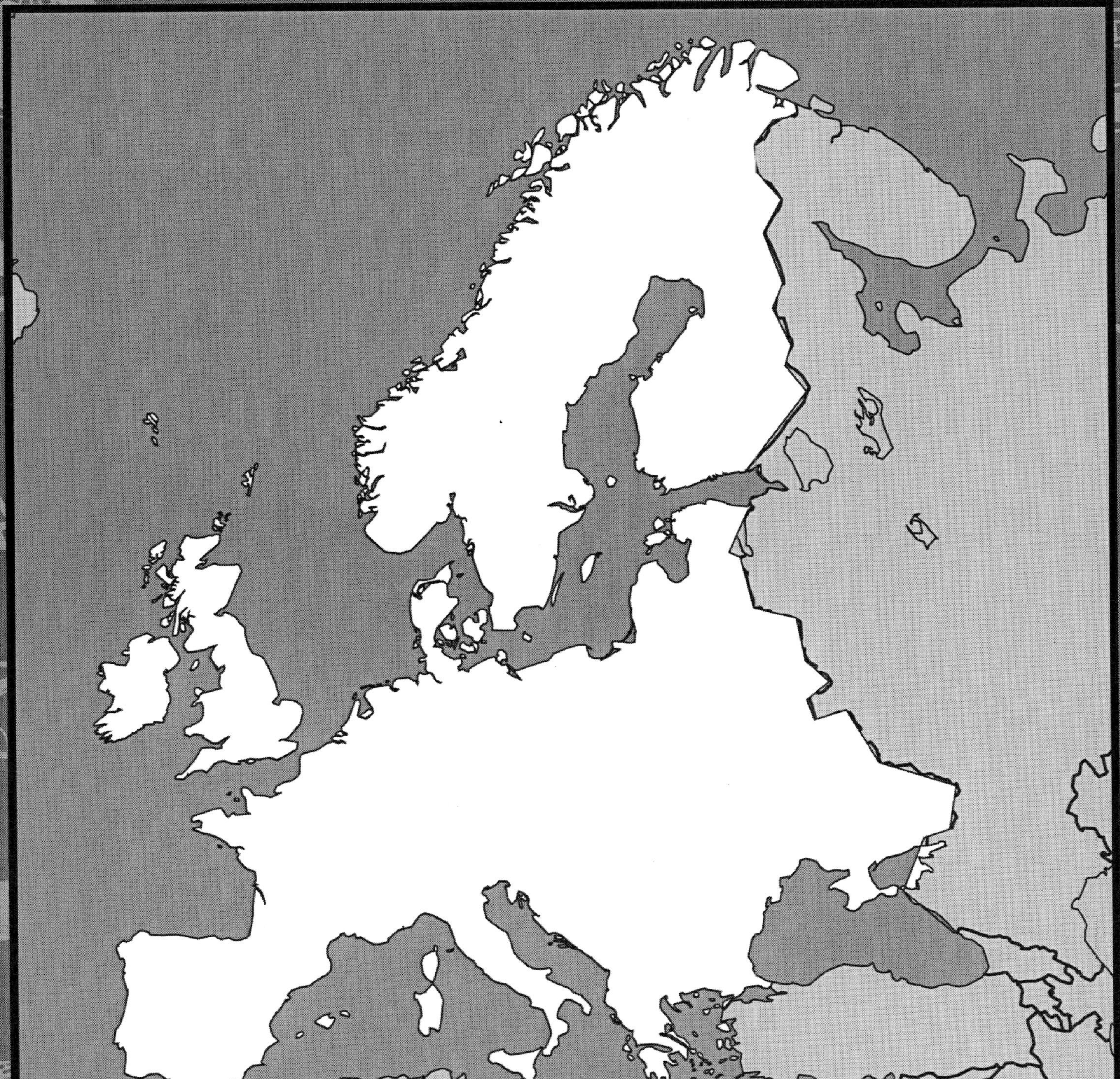

Europe
Eastern Region

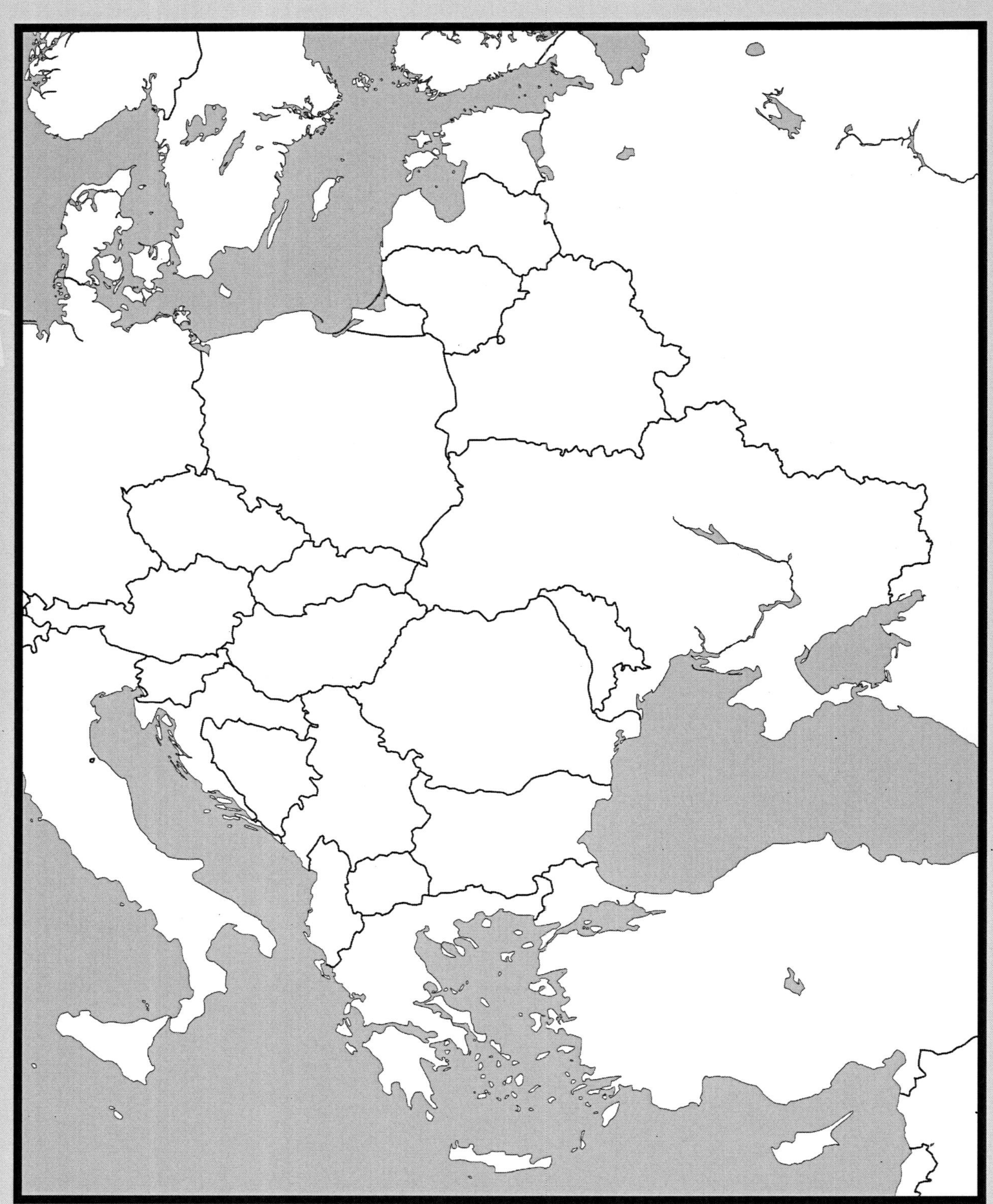

Europe
Western Region

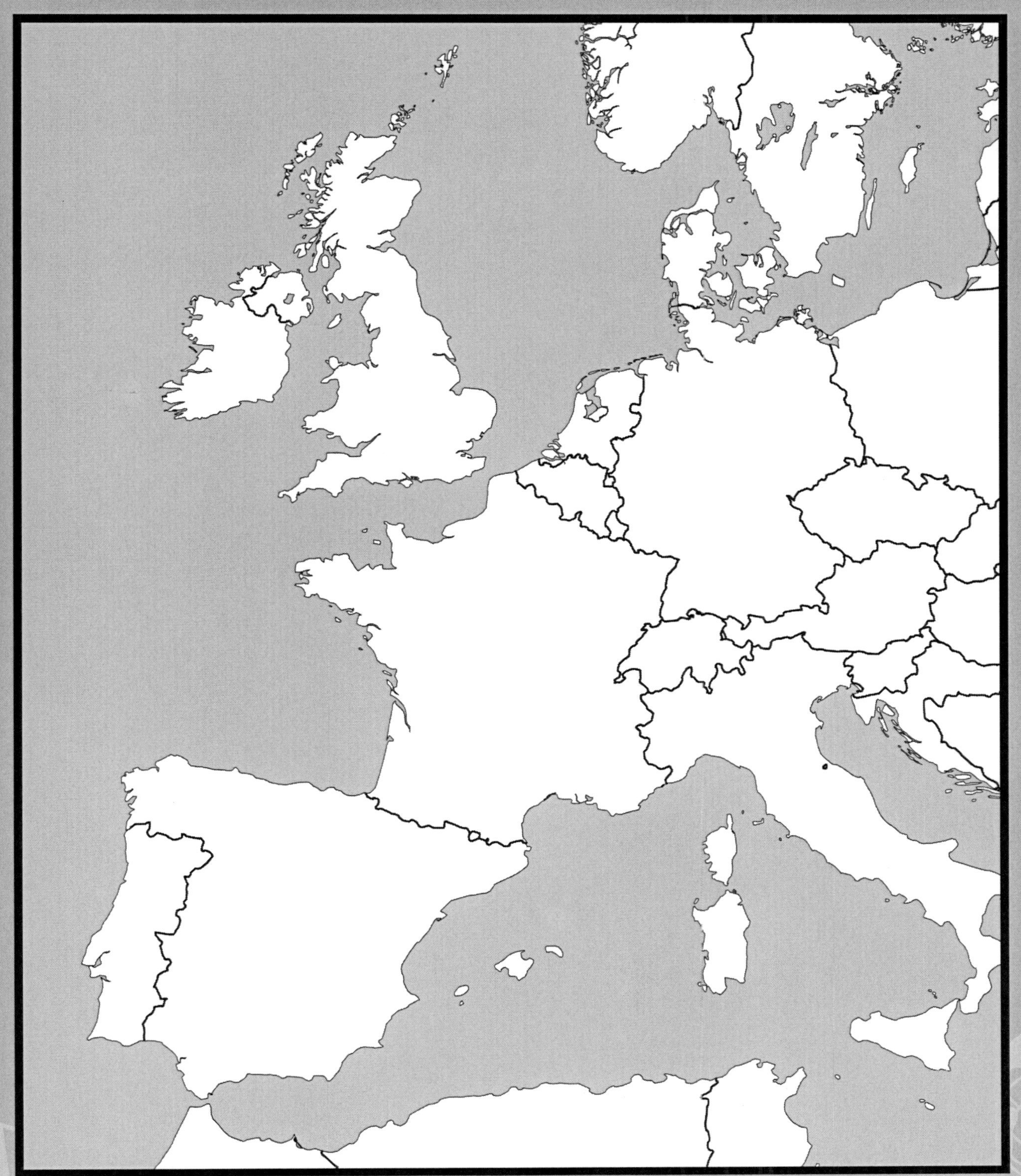

Europe
Northern Region

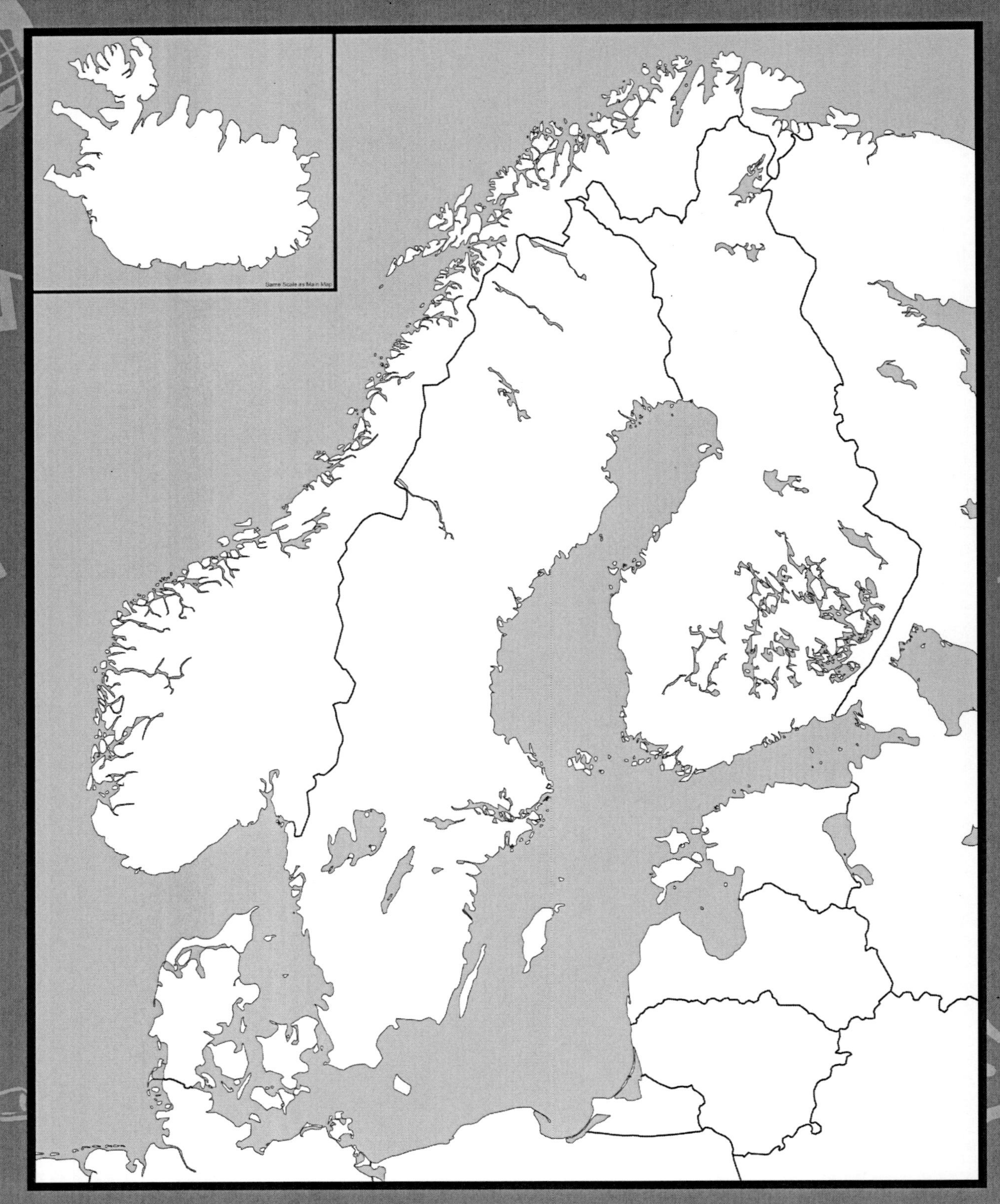

Europe World Location Map

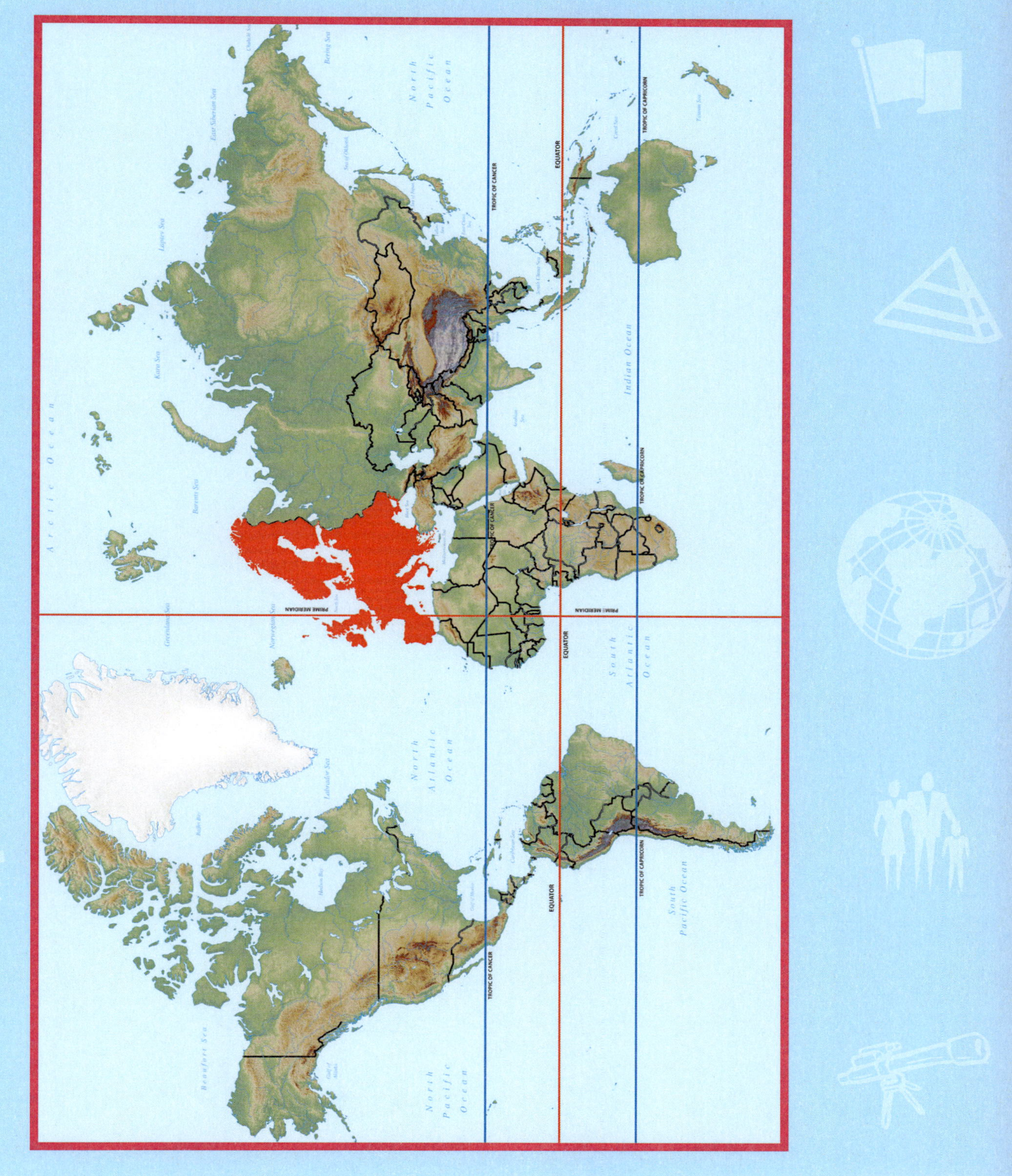

Europe Globe View Map

Europe Outline Map

Europe Physical Map

Europe Major Population Map

Europe Political Map

Europe Transportation Map

Europe Waterway Map

Europe Climate Map

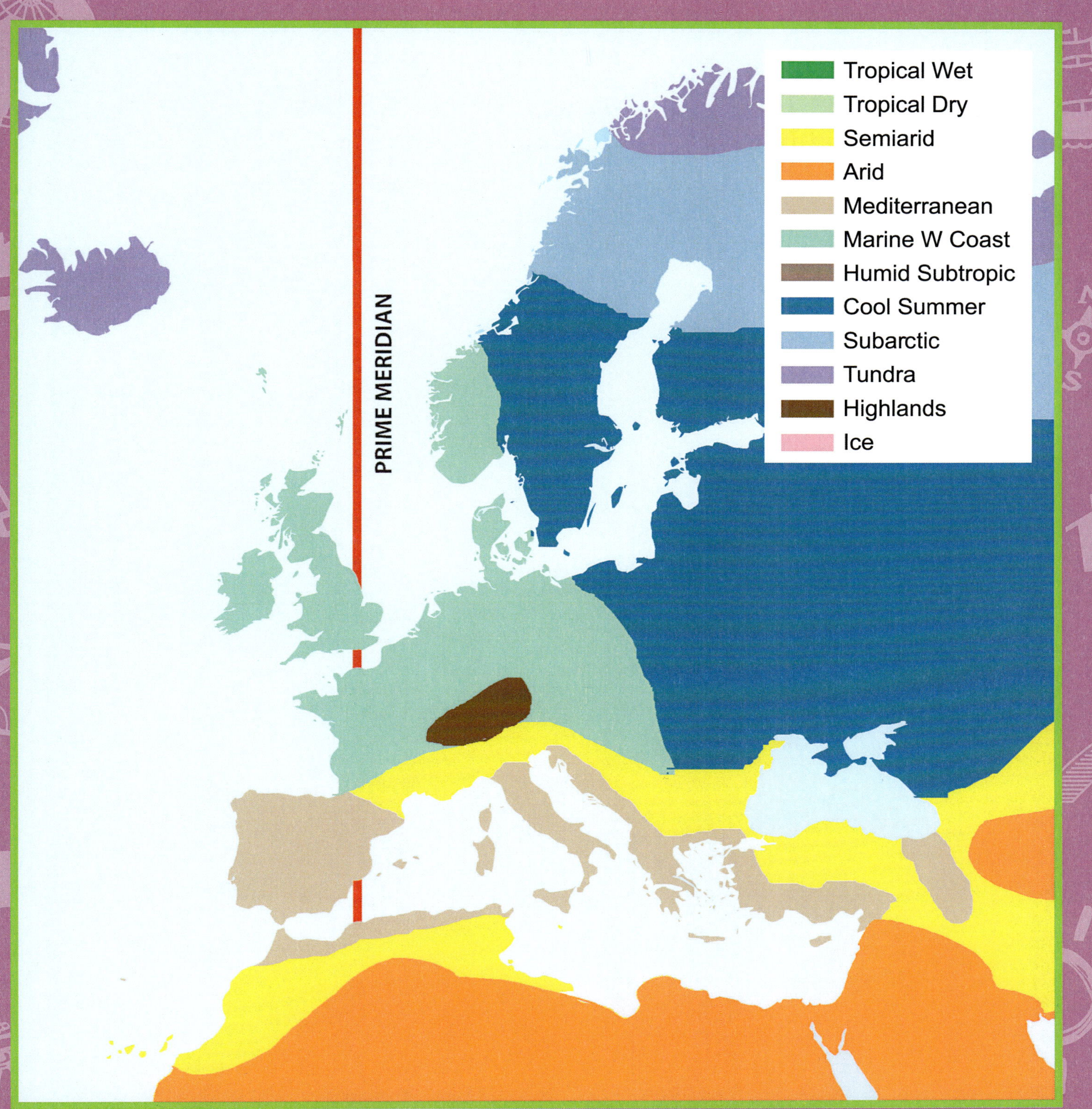

Europe
Eastern Region

Europe Western Region

Europe
Northern Region